Contents

*John Fenton and
Michael Hare Duke*

Good News

SCM PRESS LTD

Unless otherwise stated, biblical quotations
are from the Revised Standard Version

334 00588 4

First published 1976
by SCM Press Ltd
56 Bloomsbury Street London WC1

© SCM Press Ltd 1976

Filmset in 'Monophoto' Times 10 on $11\frac{1}{2}$ pt by
Richard Clay (The Chaucer Press), Ltd, Bungay, Suffolk
and printed in Great Britain by
Fletcher & Son Ltd, Norwich

Introduction

This book originated with a series of lectures delivered by John Fenton on the title 'What is the gospel?' to the Chichester Diocesan Annual Conference. Here the New Testament theology was set out. It seemed that they opened the way to a second stage of thinking in terms of pastoral practice. As parish priest and bishop Michael Hare Duke has tried to face the question 'If this is the gospel what sort of church life could give it expression?' The two ingredients have been stirred together to make what we hope is a practical recipe for church life today.

We do not expect that what we have produced will be the chart by which the churches set their course into the future. There is plenty of room for disagreement about the conclusions we have reached. What we are convinced about is the need for a fresh look at the inter-action between the way that the New Testament is understood today and contemporary patterns of church life.

There has been much recent criticism of the gulf between the work of academic theologians and the task of those who try to build up the institutional church. Radical scholars have been caricatured as dismantling the faith over against loyal parish priests who are trying to serve it up in nourishing form to the Sunday congregation or the confirmation class.

This is a false opposition, damaging equally to scholarship and pastoral practice. We hope that our small piece of co-operation may encourage others to try bridging this gulf and find authentic new ways for the gospel to be embodied in our generation.

John Fenton
Michael Hare Duke

1 · Hunt the Gospel

'Good News' as the name for a brand of chocolates is presumably considered to have sales appeal. It suggests that for your money you will get something which is attractive in taste or valuable as food. There is a hint of freshness or discovery as well that implies something you will want to pass on as information.

Long before the chocolate manufacturers, Christians were busy seeking to attract hearers by the promise of 'Good News', or gospel. People must have been expected to understand roughly the same things from the title. At the present time all the churches, at least in the West, seem to be reporting problems of decline in man power, money and ministry, so one is tempted to ask whether the news has grown stale or turned out to be bad. Or is it failing to get across in the way it deserves?

When people from the churches sit down together and discuss this kind of topic there is a danger that all attention is focussed on the means of communication. A parish conference will come up with recommendations for brighter hymns, livelier services or better vicars! One seldom finds that people have gone back to the beginning and asked themselves what the gospel really is.

Perhaps the answer seems to be too obvious; surely it is there in the pages of the New Testament. Well, so it may be, but we have to ask just exactly how we find it out. When the resources of modern scholarship are brought in to tackle the question the problem gets less easy to solve. The ordinary Christian begins to lose his nerve and landmarks which he took for certainties are called in question.

The Bible presents us with a number of gospels, or versions of Good News. There are those according to Matthew, Mark, Luke and John. Immediately we run into a problem: are the authors of the gospels the men we hear of elsewhere in the New

Testament – Matthew the tax collector who became one of the Twelve; Mark the companion of Peter and Paul; Luke the doctor and John the son of Zebedee, another of the Twelve? A widely-held view is that the authors of Matthew's gospel and John's gospel were not apostles; 'Mark' was in any case probably the commonest name in the first century; and there is a great deal of debate about 'Luke'. A suggestion made over a century ago and still very popular is that Mark's gospel was written first, and that the authors of Matthew and Luke used it; they wrote because they wanted to replace Mark with something better: something that would say what a gospel-book was meant to say, in a fuller and clearer way than the earliest gospel. Both of them add to Mark, but they also rearrange the order of incidents, and alter the way in which the narrative and the sayings are reported.

John's gospel may have been written last; it is certainly very different from the other three, and stands on its own in many respects. Its author seems to have intended to correct, and to improve upon, what had been written in other gospels.

But before any of these gospels were written, Paul was talking about 'my gospel', and he meant something quite different from the four books; he meant the message about Jesus and God, and the particular way in which he preached it.

There is therefore no simple way of fitting the four gospels and Paul's together, to make one gospel. It is a case of different wrappings, and differently-shaped chocolates. If we push the analogy further, there is even a variety of fillings. But is there some basic content that can be identified as essentially *the* Good News?

Maybe that sounds a disrespectful way to talk of holy scripture and perhaps you are wondering whether to shut the book in case it turns out to be written by some of those modern theologians who worry you by seeming to disbelieve half that the New Testament says. Wait for a moment. There is considerable reassurance in the method which we intend to pursue. If the gospel is to be found by adding together all the words which are written in the various gospels, then we are faced with an impossible task of juggling them all to fit into a unified pattern. But if we can accept that each one is a variation on a theme, a rich and colourful embroidery worked according to the vision and the temperament of the different gospellers upon one essential vision, then our problem is simpler. We need not be afraid if some particular gospel incident stretches our personal credulity too far or a commentator suggests that the words of a parable have got turned into an account of an actual event. To reinterpret individual expressions of good news will not shake or destroy the solid foundation of a faith based in the gospel itself. There is room for a great deal of uncertainty about the accuracy of the gospels as reports of what happened, without any question being involved of the truth of the gospel. Since we are seeing more and more that individual incidents in the gospels are not reliable if they are treated as eye-witness accounts of what happened, it is important that we should know what their real purpose is. We must discover the gospel to which they bear witness. This is an activity undertaken not to weaken faith but to give it a surer foundation.

So if we are looking behind the various forms of expression to the heart of the Christian good news, what is the thing for which we are seeking? What positive clues have we to guide us?

In the earliest days of Christianity, people evangelized by word of mouth. The gospel must therefore have been something that could be put into words and communicated orally; it must have been a message. When, at a later date, there were evangelistic writings, they were still composed of words and sentences, and constituted a message.

Does this mean that when we ask 'What is the gospel?' we are looking for a single form of words which we can all agree is the gospel? Will the answer to the question be a formula, which is the common factor in all the different statements of the gospel that have been made, in the New Testament, and beyond? If this were the case, we should have to consider various possible definitions, and decide which one could rightly be called the gospel. The kind of statement that might be a candidate would be, 'Jesus is Lord'; 'Christ died for our sins'; 'God is love'.

It does not seem to us that this is the right procedure. Although the gospel depends on words to communicate it, we are not going to unearth one nugget of pure gold to which we can draw your attention and say 'This is it!'. There are two reasons why this is so. First, the various ways in which the gospel has been preached, from the first days onwards, cannot be reduced to one formula, or expressed in one sentence, or even a series of

3

sentences. There is no common factor that can be neatly extracted. Secondly, the preaching of the gospel did not begin with a single formulation, from which all the later aspects of preaching were developments. The idea that it happened in this way was popular some years ago but the more you think about it the less likely it seems. From the first people were bound to preach the gospel independently, in their own way; hence the variety of theologies in the New Testament. Therefore it is not possible to trace a single statement, behind their various statements, and call it the gospel.

If, therefore, the gospel is a message that can be communicated in words, orally or in writing, and if there is no one formulation of this message, then the position clearly is that there are varieties of expression of the gospel, but no single verbal archetype.

Certainly this is how it seems to have happened: Jesus preached the gospel in one set of terms, Paul in another, John in another and so on. There are many different instances of the gospel being preached, but the gospel itself is not any one of these instances, nor even another statement like them. One could think of many other situations that are similar to this; for example there are many jokes, but there is no such thing as *the* joke; there are beautiful things, and many beautiful people, but there is nothing we can point to and say, 'That is beauty.'

It may be the case, therefore, that the question, 'What is the gospel?' is not the right question to be asking. If we start looking for a statement which is the common factor in all expressions of the gospel, or the historical basis of them all, we shall find ourselves led into a dead-end, because we shall never unearth such a magical formula. In our search we shall probably meet with a number of varying statements. It will not be a question of choosing one as the winner and discarding the others. Each will have to be evaluated against the notion of gospel to see whether it legitimately fits.

In a laboratory it is possible to conduct certain tests on a piece of metal to discover if it really is gold. We want to suggest that in the same way a set of tests can be devised which will make it possible to try out various expressions of good news and ask whether they really are the same as the gospel we find in the New Testament. This is a highly practical exercise which must con-

4

cern every minister and lay person who finds him or herself as a spokesman for the Christian church.

Although the gospel is conveyed by words, it does not stop there. Part of its truth when everything has been said about the words used to convey the good news is witnessed by the lives of the people who have shared it. We must ask what effect it had on them and whether it changed the way that they treated their neighbours. The gospel cannot be understood apart from the nature and experience of the believing community, the church. Today people ask not so much for a set of words but the demonstration of the gospel. They look at the church and ask themselves 'Is it good news?' So if we are to be practical we must centre our enquires upon the effect that any beliefs may have.

In our discussion of the gospel we intend to move from the essential marks which we discover from the New Testament to snapshots of the church here and now, in the life of the congregation which perhaps we may recognize as something like our own or to the vision of what the community of the faithful might be if we took the gospel more seriously and allowed it to form us. You can play games for ever delving into the language of the New Testament, but a gospel, if you give it your commitment, demands to be lived.

2 · Dead or Alive?

'Now look at St Vitus, there's a live church! There's always something happening in their social life. Look how active they are in the community; the things they do are always getting into the local newspaper. I believe they have tackled the whole business of finance very efficiently too. There's a business committee which has a real grip on things. They have a stewardship renewal campaign every three years and of course they've done marvels with their investments.'

'You're right, but it wasn't always like that. Before the present vicar came about six years ago they were just holding on by the skin of their teeth. It's he who got them to brighten up the services and redecorate the church. He's really put St Vitus on the map.'

Maybe we've heard that kind of conversation about a 'live church'. Maybe some of the clergy dream that it might be said about their own parish or congregation.

All of us, clergy or laity, who belong to any branch of the institutional church must in some sense want it to be a success, recognized as a going concern. But somewhere there's a nagging doubt about what those ideas really mean when applied to the church. A successful golf club is clearly one where the members are satisfied and the accounts balance. It has a limited aim and the steward has no brief to ask the members' committee whether they have got their priorities right when they decide to buy a new carpet for the bar. Disturbing issues which might cause some of the members to withdraw their subscription are quite rightly avoided by those who want to keep the harmony of the organization. That does not seem to be quite the model which we are looking for when it comes to the Christian church. Perhaps there we have to build into the expectation of a 'live church' that there will be conflict in it just because it is living. If that is the case, then has the church resources for handling this in a different way from other human institutions? Much of the time it seems that as Christians, people try to avoid disagreement, feeling that somehow that is what their faith demands. Maybe we have to reconsider whether success is to be understood in terms of bringing difficult issues out into the open rather than preserving harmony by avoiding them.

Even in the days of the first Christians, there seems to have been some doubt about what a lively church really meant. There is the comment on the church at Sardis in the Book of Revelation: 'I know your works; you have the name of being alive, and you are dead' (Rev. 3.1). Perhaps their membership numbers were up that year, perhaps they had lavishly entertained the visiting missionaries and made an extremely generous contribution towards their maintenance for the future, perhaps they had subscribed for the purchase of beautiful new onyx cups for the communion and altogether were feeling very pleased with themselves indeed. And then they read the seer's condemnation. How unfair it must have seemed. After all, it required considerable courage and committment to belong to the new, and often persecuted, sect. What more was being asked of one if all they had done was not enough? Perhaps with less justification the congregation of St Vitus might share the same feeling if they thought they were not being appreciated. But in fact are they, for all their success, a valid expression of the gospel – and by what criteria can we make any judgment?

It may be easier to tackle that question by going back a stage in our thinking. Although it has become clear that the church must always express the gospel in its life, the first communication of the Good News was in fact its proclamation in word. The church still exists to be the place where that Word is preached and what is said there must create the kind of life that flows from it. So as a first step, let us examine the content of the Sunday morning sermon, which some of us must hear and some of us must preach. When it urges us to do things, to adopt attitudes in society, reform the church this way or that, or to see ourselves in one light or another, how do we know whether it is the gospel we are hearing? When we approve of the preaching is it because it makes us feel good? When we dislike what we hear are we rejecting the preacher's errors or the Word of God?

7

Let us at this stage try to draw up a list of preliminary tests which might be applied on such an occasion to determine if what we are hearing is the gospel. For tests there must surely be, just as we can judge whether something is a joke by the criterion of whether or not it makes us laugh.

Here then by way of a start are five marks which we believe distinguish the gospel. They certainly are not the whole answer to our enquiry but they will provide a foundation upon which to build. Let's close our eyes, imagine the script of a sermon in front of us and then apply the questions, rather like chemicals being tipped one after another on to a piece of metal to test its claim to be pure gold.

1. The first test is, Is this new? The gospel is good news, and it will always have the quality of novelty about it; the man who hears the gospel always responds with surprise, 'I had never thought of that before.' This will not be because he had not heard it before, but because though he *had* heard it, he had forgotten it, and forgotten that he had heard it. The gospel comes as news, every time it is heard; and if it does not sound new, then either it is not being heard, or else it is not the gospel. This is because the gospel is heard by people who are sinners, that is to say, by people who have blotted the gospel out of their minds. Or, to put it in another way, the gospel can only be received and held on to for a moment; therefore, every time it is heard, it is as if it had never been heard before; that is why it is always new. There is a parallel with the way that beauty always comes as a fresh disclosure. We do not say of the trees in autumn, 'It is just like last year, all over again,' but we are astounded every time it happens; our favourite actresses do not so much repeat the performance whenever we see them, but surprise us by their excellence which is ever new. So one essential test of the gospel is, Is it new?

This is why the first recorded reaction to Jesus, in Mark's account, is when people remark on the novelty of what he said: 'He taught them as one who had authority, and not as the scribes . . . They were all amazed, so that they questioned among themselves, saying, 'What is this? A new teaching!' (Mark 1.22–27). And the question that Paul provokes among the Athenians in the narrative in Acts is similar; 'May we know what this new teaching is which you present?' (Acts 17.19). Paul himself found that being a Christian made it inevitable that he looked back on the scriptures on which he had been brought up as 'the old covenant' (II Cor. 3.14), a description that no Jew would ever have used; the new thing, that is, the gospel, has made what was there before now seem old (cf. Heb. 8.13).

2 . The second test is, Is it scandalous? Does it offend? The gospel is an affront to the way we live, and upsets the things we take for granted. If what claims to be a preaching of the gospel is not offensive, then it is not the gospel. One description of the gospel is that it is the Word of God, and his thoughts are not like our thoughts but contrary to them. Anything which seems to be in line with the way we automatically tend to think ought to make us suspicious as to whether it really is the gospel.

That is why Mark says that when Jesus taught in the synagogue in his own country, many were astonished and took offence at him (Mark 6.1ff.); and why Jesus says that anyone who does not take offence at him is blessed (Matt. 11.6; Luke 7.23); and why Paul says that he preaches Christ crucified, which is a stumbling block to Jews (I Cor. 1.23). The gospel strikes us first as offensive; it takes faith to receive it.

3. The third test for the gospel is, Is it excessive? The gospel is greater than our hopes, and worse than our fears. It exceeds our expectations in all directions; too good to be true, and too bad to be true. It demands that we grow in order to receive it, because it is more than we can take in. It seems incredible, and to demand the maximum of trust and surrender and self-abandonment. It goes beyond what seems reasonable and fair. It demands of us more than we can do.

Jesus never speaks in terms of a tithe as the way to measure what is claimed, or any other fraction of one's possessions (Matt. 23.23ff. and Luke 11.42 are no exception). His instruction to the rich man is to sell what he has, and give to the poor (Mark 10.21); his invitation to the disciples is to lose their lives for his sake and the gospel's (Mark 8.35). In the same way, nothing could surpass his promises: to have the kingdom, to inherit the earth, and to see God (Matt. 5.1ff.). The excess of the gospel is apparent in the saints; obvious examples are Antony of Egypt and the Desert Fathers in their extremely austere manner of life; Francis of Assisi in his poverty and love; Joan of Arc in her courage and patriotism; the Curé d'Ars in his zeal. Saints are

9

extraordinary people, because the gospel that they live by leads them to excess.

4. The fourth of these tests is, Does it bring joy? The gospel is not only news, scandalous and excessive news, but also good news. If we believed it, we would be set free from everything that makes us sad: from fear and dismal thoughts. If there could be no joy in what we heard, then what is heard is not the gospel.

The man in Jesus' parable of the treasure sells all that he has in his joy (Matt. 13.44). Paul puts joy second only to love in his account of the fruit of the Spirit (Gal. 5.22). The typical convert to Christianity hears the gospel, is baptized, and goes on his way rejoicing (Acts 8.35ff; cf. 16.34). G. K. Chesterton, in a famous passage, suggested that joy was the secret of Jesus:

> There was something that he hid from all men when he went up a mountain to pray. There was something that he covered constantly by abrupt silence or impetuous isolation. There was something that was too great for God to show us when He walked upon earth; and I have sometimes fancied that it was His mirth.[1]

There have indeed been forms of Christianity that have been utterly miserable, but they have been the aberrations; the genuine article is distinguishable by the presence of joy, one of the essential and necessary marks of sanctity.

5. The last test for the gospel is, Does it promote love? The gospel brings release from the slavery of self-centredness, and opens out the possibility of living for others. It is freedom to love – which is what we are made for. Anything that claims to be the gospel but does not and could not promote love, would not be the gospel.

Jesus made it clear that the demand of God is love (Mark 12.28ff.) and Paul said exactly the same (Rom. 13.8ff.), and put it first in the list of fruits of the Spirit (Gal. 5.22; cf. I Cor. 13). It is impossible to improve on Augustine of Hippo's maxim: 'Love, and do what you will.'

What exactly have we achieved? No definition of the gospel has emerged but it is becoming clearer what we might expect to happen when the gospel is preached and received. In such circumstances, people hear something that they think they have never heard before; something that says No to the way they are living and goes beyond all reasonable expectations; but they know that if they could believe it they would be joyful and they would be free to love. Where this is the case those people and the church they form are undoubtedly living and not dead.

3 · Upside Down

Bolted to the outside wall of the parish church at Dowally in Perthshire is an iron clamp designed to fit round a person's neck. This was the place of punishment to which a parishioner could be consigned by authority of the Kirk Session. The offence might be no more than being a gossip or a scold. It was only in the last century that this form of church discipline was abandoned after a particularly tragic incident ending in the death of the victim. Being short of stature, she had been stood on a box so that her neck reached the iron hoop. In fury at the indignity she kicked the support from under her feet and was hanged.

This story presents us with a picture of a church community determined to enforce its standards. We could certainly agree that the response had some marks of excess about it, but few people would think they saw in it an expression of the gospel.

But before we are too critical of that Perthshire Kirk Session we ought to examine less obvious ways in which Christian people consider themselves justified in imposing an ethical system upon others in the name of the gospel.

The present social climate of rapid change brings with it conflicts over moral attitudes and a great deal of uncertainty on ethical matters such as private property, work, authority, convention, the family, abortion, sex. Some people would like to see the church identify itself with movements on behalf of law and order, decency, the condemnation of pornography and so on. But the danger in this is that the church exists for the gospel, and the gospel is not the preaching of law and order; to identify the church with these movements is to make it an agent of moralism, which is not what it is meant to be.

We need to be very clear what the gospel is, before we start demonstrating, as its exponents, on behalf of some of the moral issues of today. The more the church identifies itself with the people who say Don't, the more it alienates those who already have done, and who are precisely those to whom its message should be good news. Jesus was not executed for preaching the law; he had something else to say and do; and it was the lawyers who hated him for it.

But if the gospel is not about moral demands, what is it saying? Are we being led into some permissive dead end in the name of New Testament radicalism? Surely if we go back to the original documents we cannot escape the notion of sin?

It is certainly true that at the heart of the four gospels there is a call for repentance, but perhaps the church has come to see that in more superficial terms than Jesus did; sin itself has been trivialized by being equated with a whole list of sins. Let us take a fresh look at the idea of repentance.

We begin with some passages in the New Testament, and the first is Mark's summary at the beginning of his account of the ministry of Jesus in Galilee:

> Now after John was arrested, Jesus came into Galilee, preaching the gospel of God, and saying, 'The time is fulfilled, and the kingdom of God is at hand; repent, and believe in the gospel' (Mark 1.14ff.).

Here it is stated as part of the gospel of God which Jesus preached, that repentance (and faith) are what is demanded of the hearer. Similarly, when Mark is describing the mission of the twelve, he says: 'So they went out and preached that men should repent' (Mark 6.12).

Again, in a passage which is in both Matthew's gospel and Luke's, Jesus says of his contemporaries, to whom he preached the gospel:

> The men of Nineveh will arise at the judgment with this generation and condemn it; for they repented at the preaching of Jonah, and behold, something greater than Jonah is here (Matthew 12.41; Luke 11.32).

Finally, in Luke's account of the Day of Pentecost, which is designed to be a classic and normative account of preaching the gospel, the multitude ask:

13

'Brethren, what shall we do?' And Peter said to them, 'Repent, and be baptized every one of you in the name of Jesus Christ for the forgiveness of your sins; and you shall receive the gift of the Holy Spirit' (Acts 2.37ff; see also 3.19; 5.31; 11.18; 17.30; 20.21; 26.20).

The appropriate response to the gospel is repentance; but we need to be clear that the primary meaning of the word is 'change of mind', an alteration of decision, rather than regret or sorrow. The Old Testament uses it in this way of God changing his mind. There is, however, very frequently the sense that the change is from an evil attitude to a good one (e.g. Joel 2.13ff; Amos 7.3 and 6).

This means that the gospel is an invitation to change your mind from one set of attitudes and intentions to another: A used to think X; then he heard the gospel; consequently he thought Y. His change of mind from X to Y was the result of hearing the gospel. Therefore part of the answer to the question 'What is the gospel?' must be: it is something that makes people change their minds. Or, if we put the question the other way and ask 'Is this the gospel?' then the answer must be, 'Only if it demands a change of mind.'

But this does not go far enough; it is inadequate as a description of the gospel in so far as it is a call for repentance. There are degrees of change of mind, just as there are degrees of change of wind. The change of mind that is involved in hearing the gospel is total, 180°. Here we are meeting, almost for the first time, an aspect of the gospel that we shall come across again: namely, totality. The demands of the gospel are total demands. The point here is that the gospel comes as a message informing you that you are totally wrong, and inviting you to change direction completely; not by a matter of degrees, but by the maximum change that is possible, a *volte face*. The gospel is a command to go into reverse.

This is one of the reasons why the gospel is always new and scandalous and excessive: its claim is unlimited. In this case it is saying that the direction in which you are facing is exactly the opposite to the way you should be going. There is no road this way, therefore turn round and go back. You are pointing the wrong way. The only thing to do is an about turn. This aspect of the gospel is found in sayings in the New Testament, such as:

'The last will be first, and the first last (Matt. 20.16); 'Blessed are you poor, for yours is the kingdom of God' (Luke 6.20); 'Blessed is the man who endures trial' (James 1.12).

Those who are least important and least successful in the eyes of the world, will be of the greatest importance in the eyes of God; they are the blessed. And *vice versa* those who are the most important and the most successful in the eyes of the world will be counted least by God. The future tense in the saying 'The last will be first' refers to the judgment of God at the end of the world. The saying is not only a prediction; its purpose is to inform, to explain what is the case. Then it invites the hearer to change his mind; that is, to repent. The invitation is to a complete change of mind, which involves putting the last in the place of the first, and the first in the place of the last.

We set out the formula: A used to think X; then he heard the gospel; consequently he thought Y. We can now simplify and improve this to: A used to think X; then he heard the gospel; consequently he thought $-X$. The gospel changes the signs, putting plusses for minuses and minuses for plusses.

For the moment let us apply it to the idea of God and see how it works out in that one instance. Later we shall pursue other examples, for if it is true at all the possibilities of its use are unlimited.

So, as the mathematicians say, 'let X equal God', or rather, to be precise, let X equal the way we think about God, our attitude to him. The gospel is an invitation to think about God in a way that is totally opposite to that in which we usually regard him. The non-gospel way of thinking about God is that he is great, powerful and holy, and therefore one to be feared. His greatness, power and holiness are directed against evil: he is therefore the enemy of all who have entertained evil, that is to say, of all sinners. He must be against them, because his nature is such that he cannot look upon evil; he can only be known by the sinner as his destroyer:

'It is a fearful thing to fall into the hands of the living God' (Heb. 10.31); 'Our God is a consuming fire' (Heb. 12.29, quoting Deut. 4.24).

On this view of God, the only hope for the sinner's survival would be by some change in himself that would make him acceptable to God. This might be done, if he could change from

15

being a sinner into being no longer a sinner; then, perhaps, he might stand in the presence of God. The recipe would be; stop sinning, and you will be all right. But there would be two difficulties about this: first, what about the sins committed in the past? The past cannot be changed; therefore sins committed in the past would be still outstanding. Secondly, is it possible to stop sinning?

Another possible approach, on this view of God, would be that God had mercifully allowed for or even provided some mechanism by which sin could be covered up so that it would not be seen; in this way the sinner could insulate himself against the holiness of God. This insulation was available, so some people held, through the Law of Moses; obedience to the Law cancelled out sin. Thus a second century rabbi, Eliezer ben Jacob, said:

> He who does one precept gains for himself one advocate; and he who commits one transgression gains for himself one accuser; repentance and good works are as a shield in face of punishment.[1]

By 'punishment' he meant the divine judgment; the hope which he held out was that the number of precepts of the Law that a man had fulfilled would exceed the number of his transgressions, and that his advocates would prevail over his accusers before the throne of God. Some acts were thought to be particularly meritorious: almsgiving, prayer and fasting, for example; they would atone for sin, and turn away God's wrath. Martyrdom, also, redeemed; and not only the martyrs themselves, but the people of Israel as a whole:

> Through them (i.e. the Maccabean martyrs) the enemy had no more power over our people, and the tyrant suffered punishment, and our country was purified, they having as it were become a ransom for our nation's sin; and through the blood of these righteous men and the propitiation of their death, the divine Providence delivered Israel that before was evil entreated.[2]

An older form of this view was that God had provided the means whereby sin was to be taken away, in the sacrifice of animals. The sinner could enter into communion with God through the offering of the sacrifices prescribed in the Law, par-

16

ticularly the sacrifice on the annual Day of Atonement (Lev. 16). The author of the Letter to the Hebrews interpreted the death of Jesus along these lines:

> For if the sprinkling of defiled persons with the blood of goats and bulls and with the ashes of a heifer sanctifies for the purification of the flesh, how much more shall the blood of Christ, who through the eternal Spirit offered himself without blemish to God, purify your consciences from dead works to serve the living God (Heb. 9.13ff.).

There are two difficulties about this. First, it is not all that obvious to us that the premise is true, and that the sprinkling of defiled persons in the way here described sanctifies for the purification of the flesh. Secondly, it seems unnecessarily complicated; God is first said to be against sinners, and then to have contrived a way to deal with them. Would it not be simpler to say, God is not against sinners, but for them? His greatness and power and holiness do not put him at enmity with men, though they think of him in this way: his greatness, power and holiness are all directed by love.

This is the gospel. It is an invitation to think about God in the opposite way to the way that he is usually regarded. Whereas he is thought of, apart from the gospel, as the enemy of sinners, now, by the gospel, he is to be thought of as their friend.

This was demontrated by Jesus. He ate and drank with tax-gatherers and sinners; he proclaimed God as Father, as the shepherd who searches for his lost sheep or the woman who sweeps the house to find her lost coin. Jesus said to a man who appeared out of the blue, let down through a roof: 'My son, your sins are forgiven' (Mark 2.5).

The gospel invites the hearer to repent, that is, to change his mind; and first and foremost this is to change his mind about God, and change it totally. God does not have to be placated by good works or sacrifice, because he is not in need of placating; he is for us.

But the non-gospel attitude to God is so strong that the change of mind cannot be maintained for more than a moment, although we hope that as we proceed in the Christian way, we will become more ready for each new reminder. But because we still remain sinners, the gospel is heard, and then it is forgotten;

17

and justification by good works reasserts itself. Therefore every time the gospel is heard it sounds new, and offensive, and excessive; but if it could be believed, it would really bring joy; and it would make love possible because no one can love unless he knows he is loved.

Repentance is something far more fundamental than the turning over a new leaf as it appears in much Christian moralizing. It is a matter of being born again, entering a totally new world. What sort of life opens up as a result of this experience? What sort of church can express it? It certainly will not be one which advances with heavy tread to impose its certainties on others, for we frequently have to discover that the convictions of ten years ago are precisely the subject of our present penitence.

T. S. Eliot listed among the gifts reserved for old age:

> And last the rending pain of re-enactment
> Of all that you have done, and been; the shame
> Of motives late revealed, and the awareness
> Of things ill done and done to others' harm
> Which once you took for exercise of virtue.
> Then fools' approval sings, and honour stains.[3]

If you believe that you will hesitate to leave the marks of your certainties upon others and you certainly will not chain them to the church wall!

4 · Perpetual Repentance

Dear Reader,

We hope that you have got this far with our book. (In fact, of course if you haven't you won't be reading this anyway, unless you are leafing through it in a bookshop, in which case how about buying a copy?) We would like you to think that it makes a great deal of sense and therefore to approve of us. To be honest we hope that reviewers will notice it and we shall look anxiously for their comments in the right papers; and if they do not give it a favourable notice we shall comfort ourselves with reflections on their lack of real appreciation.

Although we believe that we wrote it because we had something to say, we would not mind finding that it turned into a best-seller and made us a handsome profit. Unfortunately there is no story-line to make it a candidate for treatment on film or TV.

Most writers do not include this kind of thing in their books but the readers attribute it to them anyway. We have come clean and so, we hope you will observe, have proved ourselves to be exceptionally open and honest.

Yours sincerely,

THE AUTHORS

It may be a bit of a caricature, but perhaps there is enough of the real situation expressed in such a letter to make it possible to use it as case material as we go on to look at the question of what repentance means in terms of ourselves and of the world.

Following the formula which we have suggested, let us say that X equals ourselves. Then apart from the gospel we think of ourselves in one way, but as a result of hearing the gospel we think of ourselves in the diametrically opposite way. How does this work out?

The non-gospel attitude sees oneself as threatened, at risk, likely to be under attack from some quarter or other. This may include God, or life, or other people, or the world, or death. Therefore one must be on the defensive, ready to ward off the enemy, and not surrender to his forces. Moreover, because the best form of defence is attack, the wisest policy is to be aggressive.

The gospel is an invitation to change one's mind totally. This will involve an entirely contrary attitude to oneself, and entirely opposite policies for one's life. It will involve thinking that neither people nor situations are against me. I need not adopt an aggressive attitude towards them nor try to establish my ascendency over them. Above all, it will mean that I am not threatened by God, because he is now seen to be for me, and not against me. And if he is for me, who is against me? Therefore the attitude of aggression against all comers can be changed into one of welcome and surrender; it will be possible to give oneself away, freely and without self-consciousness. For it is the mark of the defensive person always to be looking over his shoulder to ask himself 'How am I doing now?'

The defensive stance seems so natural to us that, here again, the gospel will always come as something new and offensive and excessive. But it will also bring joy and make love possible: it will be release from fear, and freedom to love.

Then, suppose we put the world into the formula which we devised, as the quantity X. Once again we find a new situation. There is a non-gospel way of thinking about the world, and there is a gospel way of thinking about the world and the two are directly contrary, the one to the other.

The non-gospel way of thinking about the world is as 'that which is not mine', because it is possessed by other people. Nevertheless, I want it, or at least as much of it as I can get. I need it in order to live; it provides me with the necessities of living: food, air, space, shelter, community and so forth. I must therefore devise and pursue ways of grasping as much of the world as I possibly can, in competition with others, who are all in the same situation, where every man is for himself or his group.

The gospel calls for a complete change of outlook, and demands a way of life which is directly contrary to this. The attitude of the gospel is summed up in such statements as:

'All things are yours' (I Cor. 3.21); 'Having nothing, and yet possessing everything' (II Cor. 6.10).

That is to say, the gospel invites us to think of the whole world as our possession, and it points out the inevitable corollary, that if the world is our possession, we need not stake out any part of it as especially our own. Because you possess everything, you need have nothing; only by having nothing can you possess everything.

The gospel thus frees a man to possess and enjoy the whole world. It frees him from taboos. The man who has not heard the gospel is afraid of certain things and calls them unclean; unclean meats, for example. But the gospel declares all meats clean (Mark 7.19). Sex is another example. The gospel removes all taboos from sex. It says that nothing is unclean in itself (Rom. 14.14). This is the glorious liberty of the children of God (Rom. 8.21) and the gospel invites you to receive it and accept it and enter into it. Every time this gospel is proclaimed, it seems to the aggressive, timid or fearful men who hear it, both new and scandalous and excessive; but also joyful; and the only possible ground for loving.

What does this kind of repentance have to say to the two authors in the context of their letter which began this chapter? Is it possible that people who are writing about the gospel could be in need of a radical reappraisal of their own attitudes?

This is the point about our insistence that the gospel continually comes as 'news'. By nature we all seem to lose sight of it as soon as it is grasped. Indeed we actually manage to turn its liberating vision into a system that imposes restrictions. In the name of the gospel one set of Christians has persecuted another. From entrenched positions they have mouthed slogans about 'free grace'; in the name of charity they have vilified the theology of others and in more extreme cases actually done them physical harm.

To preserve a truth it seems that we need to formalize it and the formula tempts us to defend it in a way that can deny the original truth. So it is all too easy to preach a sermon or write a book about the openness of the gospel and be found anxiously defending your particular set of words or flaunting them in the face of an opponent. And where is the gospel then?

If this is true of the individual, it is also true of the church as a whole. In every denomination we have inherited good things from the past, but we do not seem to be very skilful in distinguishing the things which were once excellent expressions of the gospel from its unchanging essence. In a world which is in the process of making a new cosmology, old survivals are in danger of becoming simply museum pieces. Repentance means discovering the growing points within the structure which we have. The gospel is to be found at the place which is capable of development and not in the rigid *status quo*.

Whenever a church faces up to the living God, it is made aware of the temptation to put its trust in lesser things, patterns of liturgy, beautiful architecture, uplifting music, a particular set of human relations or forms of theology. All may be necessary ingredients in setting a course towards God, but none must ever take the place of God. So a faith in God means that there is a built-in expectation of change which arises out of a response to growth.

The church must be organized to make contact with the world in which it operates. It will have to express its life in terms of the prevailing culture. Certainly this has happened in the past. In a feudal society the church adopted the pattern of episcopacy which saw the bishop as a spiritual parallel to the temporal lord. After the industrial revolution the prevailing entrepreneurial structures were again initiated by the church as the missionary societies were founded to export the gospel, or to market Christian education. The bureaucratic age has seen the proliferation among all the denominations of their various secretariats and the World Council of Churches parallels the United Nations. The trouble is that history tends to sanctify these structures and instead of one replacing another they lie uneasily alongside, like salmon on a fishmonger's slab, and only painfully achieve any inter-relation. We lack the courage to leave behind us patterns which though once good now no longer serve the cause of the kingdom. We hold on to them as things valuable in themselves.

Now this is the very antithesis of the life of the gospel. 'The sabbath was made for man, not man for the sabbath', said the Lord, pushing out of his way a sacred cow which blocked the path of honest human development.

The demand for 'repentance' is the demand that we shall be

able to look openly at anything and evaluate it in the light of God's continuing purpose. We have to be ready to come clear of even our former 'righteousness', because it too becomes a trap that negates the possibility of growth.

Sometimes the call to move on comes from the outward events but there is also an inner compulsion to change in response to growth. For instance how do people actually become Christians? For some it happens because of a particular set of relationships; a person may have been brought up as part of a church family, or perhaps as a teenager he began to go with friends to some kind of Christian organization. Someone else may have grown up within the aura of a particular religious allegiance, a Catholic or Protestant in Ulster, and be held to it by cultural pressures.

Development in the life of the Spirit is bound to require movement from such positions, whether it be gradual or sudden. To remain static is either to lapse into empty formalism or to become bigoted, defending one's position with all the force of internal anxiety. The gospel sets us free to look again at what we are doing and to move on from any pattern of devotion or any stereotyped way of living that has reduced the message of love into a demand for conformity.

If this is true, we must realize that whenever we start to look for an 'ideal church' we are bound to be wrong. For by definition, there can only be a temporary resting place, and after that the journey must continue.

The same thing happens in family life. As the children grow and develop as individuals, they impinge in new ways on their parents. This demand for a new response will only be achieved by the older generation at some emotional expense. Love responds quite differently to the tears of a three-year-old, and to the frustration of a teenager. But sometimes parents want to keep things as they were. It seems too difficult to see the relationship in a new light, although for both parties this can be a creative, learning situation. Any attempt to hold things back and pretend that nothing is changing represents a neurotic refusal to face reality. The new awareness, the reversal of previous attitudes, the willingness to accept the past mistakes are all part of a healthy development.

The same is true for the church when it is obedient to the gospel, and it finds the same resistance to change. The gospel with the call to move on is offensive. Every pilgrim seems bound to wish that the present oasis could become 'home'.

But the very heart of the gospel is the demand for repentance, the total change of mind, the complete alteration of direction from the non-gospel point of view. As we have looked at these three points, the objection may have arisen that this is all very well, but it is totally impractical. Would it not be prudent to retain some fear of God, and to think of him as one who might eventually condemn us? Would it not be useful to keep an element of aggression and ambition to get on in the world, and succeed? Must we not retain our right to private property, in order to live? Surely the church must not disturb people too much by its change of ways. If this is the gospel, then the gospel is impractical.

Perhaps we have here another test, to add to the five which we listed above: if we want to know whether what we have heard is the gospel, then it is essential that what we have heard should seem impractical. This must be so because it is the gospel of God, and his thoughts are not our thoughts, nor are our ways his.

5 · Models in the Melting Pot

In 1861 the Reverend George Howard Wilkinson, a sincere young clergyman in his late twenties, was the vicar of Seaham Harbour in Co. Durham.

The parish to which this young priest, later to be Bishop of Truro and then of St Andrews, was presented at the age of twenty-six was a tough assignment. His Edwardian biographer describes it as 'a rather bleakly situated town on the North-East coast, seven miles south of Sunderland, with a population at that time of about 6,000 consisting of bottle makers, iron founders, miners, sea-faring folk and agents of the Londonderry Estate' (*Memoir of George Howard Wilkinson* by A. J. Mason, DD).

His vigorous ministry quickly began to take effect. A parish which had always known only a single incumbent found itself with a staff of vicar and two curates and the Sunday congregation increased so considerably that an enlargement of the church became necessary and an aisle was added giving accommodation for two or three hundred more worshippers.

The basis of George Wilkinson's ministry was sound teaching. To illustrate this the *Memoir* quotes 'A characteristic paper headed in large letters:

SEARCH THE SCRIPTURES

We are told to search the Scriptures. The following are a few of the truths which will be found in the Scriptures if they are so searched:

1. God is holy and true and just.
2. God has given us a law.

3. We have broken this law.

4. We are guilty in God's sight and can never have real happiness till we are pardoned.

5. We can never obtain this pardon or put ourselves right with God by any thing which *we* ourselves can do.

6. God has provided a way by which we can be pardoned. He has given His own Son to suffer the punishment for our sins by dying for us.

7. God offers to pardon us *at once* if we turn from our sins and believe in Jesus Christ. When we believe we are *justified*, that is, acquitted.

8. It is not enough to be *acquitted*. We have a bad heart which must be made good before we can enter into Heaven. The Holy Spirit alone can do this for us. This is what the Bible means by *sanctification*.

9. The Holy Spirit's help is promised to us if we earnestly pray for it.

10. The real Christian must be always trying to become better.

11. He must often ask God for what he wants in prayer.

12. He must often study his Bible.

13. He must *regularly* attend the public worship of God and not be absent from the Lord's Supper.

14. He must be holy, meek, ready to forgive, humble, charitable, self-denying, obedient to the *law* of the country and to his parents, trying in every way to follow Jesus Christ's example.

15. He must confess Christ before man.

16. He must try to bring others to Jesus and do some work for the Church of Christ.

Seaham Harbour, 1861'

Each of these propositions is illustrated in the leaflet by a number of appropriate texts.

Throughout his ministry the good Bishop was in the habit of writing such authoritative documents, including, under the direction *How to live a Christian Life*, the stern injunction: 'Do not run about from one church to another; keep to your own church. Never go to chapel.'

The interesting thing is not only that the Bishop felt he could write such things with complete confidence but also that such bald statements appear to have proved an effective vehicle of mission. The good news was for him reducible to a clear set of practical propositions which appealed to a basis of texts in scripture.

Today, as one reads the biography, there are objections at three levels. First the world in which we live no longer accepts such authoritative pronouncements unchallenged. Secondly biblical scholarship would question whether the dogmatic statements that the Bishop makes could be maintained. Thirdly the psychologically-informed reader is likely to connect the high degree of personal demand contained in his formulation of the gospel with the fact that throughout his life, he had to withdraw for recuperation after periods of complete exhaustion and that finally his episcopate at Truro ended in a depressive breakdown.

Writing less than seventy years ago the pious biographer, the Revd Arthur James Mason, had no hint of such questions in his mind. It is the measure of the change through which we have passed in this century that such a gulf exists between ourselves and him. Almost every assumption by which our grandparents lived is now capable of reappraisal. In morals and metaphysics questions have replaced certainties. A new concept of authority has changed the underlying pattern of education and of politics. Scientific invention has altered our ideas of what is humanly possible and the behavioural sciences have given us new eyes with which to look at man and his motives.

Since Christians are part of this world of questioning it is not surprising to find the church also looking for its bearings. The awareness of how much we have in the past been conditioned by the culture which is shared with the world around may make a church all the more ready to go back to its first principles in the New Testament.

Suppose that a thoughtful diocese should invite a distinguished New Testament scholar to come amongst its clergy and help them re-explore the nature of the gospel. Can we imagine what effect it would have had if his response had been in some of the terms set out in the preceding chapters? He would doubtless have received an attentive hearing, but what then?

The scene is set at a conference centre where the clergy of the diocese are gathered. The sun shines, the trees and the grass are green. As they pace up and down the lawn, a group of dedicated parish priests express themselves deeply disappointed in what has been said.

'Definite teaching is what we need,' a senior canon is grumbling, 'people don't want airy fairy ideas. Imagine trying to get that kind of stuff over to a confirmation class.'

'I agree, I've tried this sort of thing in Lent discussion groups, and it's always been a failure,' chimes in another determined-looking cleric. 'People know that we have got a training in theology, and they want us to tell them what the faith really is, not ask them questions or stand everything on its head.'

'It's all very well for these scholars to say they're not very sure about the apostolic preaching, but people respond to hard facts.'

Sitting in the sun-lounge, we find another dissident group, the administrators.

'Well, he more or less admitted that it is impractical, and if somebody doesn't pay the quota, keep the roof on and find the stipend, then there will be no church left in which to bandy these or any other ideas!'

'You've got to start where you are and the fact is that we have inherited tremendous assets from the past. We have got our buildings; we have got our connections weaving out into society. The job of the church leader today is to take all these things and to give them new impetus. Don't get me wrong, I'm not in favour of secularizing the gospel, but really we would do better to ask a market research man to look at what people are saying and thinking and then see how we could meet what they want, rather than exhausting ourselves by going back to these paradoxical first principles!'

'Of course,' said the Archdeacon to the Suffragan Bishop over a quiet gin, 'you couldn't run a diocese on these assumptions. It's all very well if you live in the ivory tower of a university to dream up such ideas, but put them into practice and you'd split the church right down the middle. What you want in a bishop is a good chairman, not someone doing excessive things. After all, that doesn't even square with his own ideal of a gospel which is "productive of love". Someone who acted in that sort of way would make people angry and frustrated. You couldn't do a pastoral job on these principles; you would have any con-

28

gregation at sixes and sevens in no time at all.

'And as for any kind of ecumenical work that we are trying to do, people would obviously lose confidence if they were negotiating with a committee which talked in this sort of way. You'd never know where you were with them.'

In the solitude of his room one might imagine the Bishop closing his Greek New Testament, to which the lectures had led him back. What did these commands imply for the kindly, faithful clergy of his diocese? The explosive force of the Lord's witness did not link easily into the steady round of church business that he saw as he visited the parishes. The Norman pillars and Gothic windows of the buildings spoke of a stability and a measured way of existence. People resisted change even in terms of church architecture. How was it possible that they should respond to a revolutionary teaching that rocked the foundations of their way of life?

The New Testament that he was using was the one that he had been given at his ordination to the diaconate. As he looked at its worn black cover he recognized that his first sermons had shown some of the insights that he had recently experienced in the lectures. With a start he began to wonder whether the concern for making the machine run smoothly had really blurred his vision so badly. Was it wisdom and prudence which guided his concern or a pragmatic awareness of what he felt people could take? Nobody wants excess or offence but do they even really want that which is new, loving and joyful?

Bishops are sometimes called 'Guardians of the Faith'. Was this New Testament faith something you guarded by careful planning or was part of its paradox that it was most faithfully preserved when it was taken seriously enough to be put at risk?

Was it possible that the church as he knew and loved it was dangerously near to denying the gospel, because it was so anxious about its own preservation?

Since bishops continually face practical situations and hopefully translate their theology into terms which help make decisions, his mind went to the last committee meeting he had attended before the conference. Much anxious thought had been given to the question of closing a church whose congregation were in deep financial difficulty. As the facts of the case unfolded it seemed that for years their loyal efforts had been directed to the one task of making financial ends meet. There was no spare energy for meeting or study to take them further into the understanding of the gospel or care of their neighbours.

It had begun to dawn on him that 'good news' for that little band of Christians might be a realization that their loyalty to that church building was mistaken. It had been built as an expression of mission and faithfulness. As circumstances had changed it had grown into an unrealistic burden. Now, if those doors were closed there might be opened a door into heaven that could transform the congregation's life together.

You would not do that by printing them a tract with scripture quotations. A way must be found of leading them back into the New Testament experiences of death and rebirth, so that they could have a new ability to change and *grow*.

As the Bishop thought of the one particular parish, he might well have reflected that what he discerned there was the necessity for himself, his diocese and indeed the whole church.

6 · Have Faith, Will Travel

Anyone who is going to take seriously the New Testament declaration that life comes out of death is not in for a comfortable time. The politician has presumably got to be ready to lose an election. The business man may have to put his career at risk. The scholar may have to go out on a limb for the truth as he sees it. The liberator may find that his path leads to the execution yard. The ecclesiastic may at least have to help congregations disband. Is this sort of conclusion too crazy to make any practical sense?

It seems to take a great deal of believing to accept such ways forward. But belief is another key word in the New Testament vocabulary. Maybe we had better go back and see what light can be shed on our practical dilemma.

'The time is fulfilled, and the kingdom of God is at hand, repent, and believe in the gospel' (Mark 1.15). Mark's summary of the preaching of Jesus contains two verbs in the indicative, and two in the imperative. Between them they state the content of the gospel, then declare what the response to it should be: repentance and faith. So now we need to get on the trail of faith and the way forward seems to be the one we have followed in order to discover what was involved in changing our mind. We shall ask what the gospel is, if what it expects of the hearer and produces in him is faith.

First of all the language needs some detailed examination. The noun 'faith', the verb 'believe', and the adjective 'faithful' are key words in the vocabulary of Christianity:

'I believe; help my unbelief' (Mark 9.24); 'He himself believed, and all his household' (John 4.53); 'All who believed were together and had all things in common (Acts 2.44); 'Men, what must I do to be saved? . . . Believe in the Lord Jesus, and

31

you will be saved, you and your household' (Acts 16.30f.).

If you wanted to talk about 'a Christian' in New Testament language you said 'a believer'. When we say 'Christianity', in the first century they said 'the faith'. The word 'Christian' only appears three times in the New Testament (Acts 11.26; 26.28; I Peter 4.16). Christianity is never mentioned at all. When Paul is writing to the Galatians he uses 'the faith' in this way. He is speaking about the time between his visit to Jerusalem after his conversion and his second visit many years later. He says:

> I was still not known by sight to the churches of Christ in Judaea; they only heard it said: 'He who once persecuted us is now preaching the faith he once tried to destroy' (Gal. 1.22f.).

If Paul is reporting the exact words that the Christians in Judaea were using at the time, we have evidence that as early as the forties of the first century 'the faith' was a term used by Christians to mean what it was that made them what they were. There is a similar use of the word further on in the same letter:

> 'Now before faith came, we were confined under the law, kept under restraint until faith should be revealed' (Gal. 3.23).

It was faith which marked the first Christians off from the Jews. The Christians were people who believed, and the Jews were people who did not. Of course there were many things that Jews and Christians believed in common; nevertheless, what divided them was, in the Christians' understanding of the matter, faith: what Christians believed and Jews did not, or perhaps it would be better to say, how Christians believed but Jews did not.

The cause of the difference between Jews and Christians was the gospel; therefore we are asking, what is the gospel, if what it produces is believers?

Part of the answer is there already: the only thing the gospel could produce would be believers. It requires a change of mind, from what is considered usual and reasonable, to what seems impractical and always strikes the hearer as new and offensive and excessive. It expects you to think about God in the opposite way to that in which people usually think about him; to change your attitude towards yourself and the world to the entire opposite from what you were brought up to think was right. For this change, something is needed which goes beyond our natural capacities and propensities; and this is faith in one of its meanings.

Take the case of a person being told something he did not know before. The news may be one of two kinds. It may be what he did not know, but he is not surprised to hear. For example, that the Russians had put a man on Mars would not be all that surprising (at least to those of us who know nothing at all about conditions on Mars). One might think that if the Americans could put a man on the moon, it would not be all that out of the way if the Russians did the same on Mars. But suppose that the news went beyond what had been thought possible, or rather, to be more precise, were contrary to everything that had been thought before. This would be really surprising and would take more accepting. Suppose that the news were that the Chinese had put a man on the sun (and he was alive and well). It had always been thought that the sun was hot, and that no one could approach it and live. This, we should say, would take some believing.

The biblical example of faith is Abraham's trust in God that he would have a son, though he was as good as dead (he was about a hundred years old), and though Sarah, his wife, was barren. Faith is what enables a man like Abraham to be fully convinced that God is able to do what he has promised, though it seems impossible (see Rom. 4.16–25).

The gospel is so incredible that the only people who accept it must be believers. Its call for repentance, for change of mind and policy, is so drastic, that it might be said of those who adopt the change, that if they believe that, they will believe anything.

But here we have got to be careful about what it is that we are saying. Faith is not about accepting a set of impossible propositions. That is to be put into a straitjacket which denies growth and development; that opposes the essential quality of exploration, of journeying, that is at the heart of faith in God.

A stark contrast illustrating these two attitudes emerges in the life of Charles Darwin, the man who changed so much of our understanding about what 'creation' means.

In 1831 when he was invited to join the survey ship HMS *Beagle* as a naturalist, he was a young man of twenty-two just down from Cambridge and destined, without much conviction, to be ordained to the ministry of the Church of England.

The captain of the *Beagle* was Robert FitzRoy. He had a special purpose in mind for this particular expedition beyond the task given him by the Admiralty.

The voyage, he believed, would provide a grand opportunity to substantiate the Bible, especially the book of Genesis. As a naturalist, Darwin might easily find many evidences of the flood and the first appearance of all created things upon the earth. He could perform a valuable service by interpreting his scientific discoveries in the light of the Bible. Darwin, the young clergyman to be, was very ready to agree. He too, did not in the least doubt the literal truth of every word in the Bible at this time – it was part of the world he accepted and liked so well – and if he could be of any use in this way, well then that made the prospect of the Voyage all the most exciting.[1]

From such a beginning, the two characters, the naval officer and the naturalist, arrived at the most divergent conclusions. As scientist, Darwin followed where the facts as he conceived them led him. His obedience was to the journey. FitzRoy by contrast held on to his conviction that the whole text of the Bible as he knew it was unerringly true. Long after the voyage of the *Beagle* was over the two men confronted each other. At the celebrated meeting of the British Association held in Oxford in 1860 not only was Samuel Wilberforce, Bishop of Oxford, there to oppose vehemently Darwin's theories of evolution and T. H. Huxley there to defend them, but amongst the audience was Vice-Admiral Robert FitzRoy holding a copy of the Bible in his hand and almost hysterically proclaiming it as the unique source of the truth. What the Admiral and the Bishop of Oxford would have identified as faith was the thing that prevented the Admiral looking at reality openly and unafraid. His world was a closed system which rejected new insights but because he used the language of religious belief its true quality was disguised. For those who saw him as a man of faith it must have been a catastrophic shock when he committed suicide five years later. There were tragic circumstances which might have seemed sufficient explanation for his action, but the fact that he saw self-destruction as the only way out of his frustration and despair is of a piece with the rigid pattern of belief which could not shift or adapt in the face of new evidence. He had decided within his own frame of reference what was believable and could not risk the invitation to grow beyond it.

The man who assented to the orthodox formula, who doubtless won the approval of Bishop Wilberforce and his clergy, now seems to us to be someone who had missed the gospel. By contrast the apparent enemy of the faith who patiently pursued the facts as he found them appears to have a greater claim to be called a man of faith. He is the one who took the risk of exploration, leaving the safety of the sheltered unquestioned assumptions.

In saying this we are making a judgment, but to what authority can we appeal for support? We have used the example of Vice-Admiral FitzRoy to illustrate the point that faith in a static document or a fixed formula is a denial of the gospel. But can we in turn be accused of setting up another equally rigid criterion? We have said that faith is a response to the gospel which demands a reversal of attitudes when it is accepted. There is not a written set of propositions which can sum up what this entails once and for all. What we can do is point to those who have believed and demonstrate the common quality of faith in their lives. This is the method adopted by the author of the Letter to the Hebrews (Heb.11.1–12.2). After the list of the Old Testament examples, all of which are concerned with a reversal of accepted values and expectations, the passage ends with Jesus 'the pioneer and perfecter of our faith'. In him the author sees the fundamental paradox of joy and the cross. His thought is paralleled by the modern song which begins from the thought of the foolishness of God (I Cor. 1.32).

> Come holy harlequin
> shake the world and
> shock the hypocrite
> Rock love, carry it away
> Turn it upside down
> Let the feast of love begin
> Let the hungry all come in
> Rock love carry it away
> Turn it upside down
> Let the rich and mighty wait

35

Let the poor go through the gate
Rock love carry it away
Turn it upside down [2]

But if faith turns things upside down how is it to be commended to a thoughtful world? What will persuade people to come out from their security to journey with Abraham or chose with Moses to be on the side of the underdog?

7 · The Witnesses

In the last chapter we were arguing that faith is expressed in an attitude to life. At the same time it has a content. We cannot live in a new way unless something has changed which makes this possible. The Christian claims that these new factors are contained in the gospel. Where this is both proclaimed and accepted something quite fresh enters the situation.

So first of all the gospel is a message. This means it requires communication. It must be passed on by word of mouth, or in writing, or in symbols, or by art. It can only be received through the ears or the eyes or touch; there is no other way of getting it. When the gospel is received, then there is faith; there is no other way of becoming a believer, except by having the gospel communicated to you. 'Faith comes from what is heard, and what is heard comes by the preaching of Christ' (Rom. 10.17).

Faith is not spontaneous, in the sense of spontaneous combustion, or spontaneous generation. No one can spark off faith by himself and in himself, apart from any outside agent; the technical term which is used in the New Testament for the person who sparks off faith in another is 'witness', and this action of producing faith in the other person is 'testimony'.

In the New Testament, a witness is not one who sees something, i.e. an observer, but one who says what he has seen or heard. The first man to be a witness to Jesus, and to testify to him, was John the Baptist: 'He came for testimony, to bear witness to the light, that all might believe through him' (John 1.7). All subsequent witnesses and evangelists and preachers have in one sense only repeated in their own way what the Baptist said first in his: 'Behold, the Lamb of God, who takes away the sin of the world' (John 1.29). So all who believe, believe through him.

Therefore when we say the gospel produces believers, we are using a shorthand expression, and omitting an element from the situation. The gospel is a message, and a message can only be communicated by means of a messenger. The gospel by itself, without somebody to proclaim it, can do nothing; it only produces believers when it is preached.

This helps to throw light on the point we have made; that the gospel is not a fixed form of words, a formula that can be learned off by heart, for repetition. It cannot be received except through a man, a witness, who must put it in his own way, the way that makes sense to him. There must be as many ways of proclaiming the gospel as there are preachers of the gospel. All that we can handle is these expressions of the gospel, never the gospel itself; we can only receive it mediated through the mind and experience of another believer, never in a direct and immediate form. (Incidentally, this is why it is unsatisfactory to preach the sermons written by somebody else; or one's own sermons written some time before, when the preacher himself was a different person.)

Faith comes from what is heard; so the gospel is a kind of invitation, inviting the hearer to become a believer. Hence the sayings of Jesus about invitations; for example: 'I came not to call the righteous, but sinners' (Mark 2.17).

The Greek word which is here translated 'call' is the word which is translated 'invite' in Luke 14, 7, 8, 9, 10, 12, 13, 16. One test for the gospel is whether there is an invitation implicit in what is being said; whether the hearer is being requested to believe something, as if he had never believed it before.

But this is an inadequate way of putting it; anyone who states a proposition of any kind invites belief, or unbelief, in the truth of what he is saying. The gospel does not only ask for belief in the truth of the gospel, it also invites the hearer to do something different, and to be a different person, because of the gospel. It invites the hearer to become a follower.

Mark sets this out in dramatic form in a story which he puts immediately after the first summary of the preaching of Jesus:

And passing along by the Sea of Galilee, he saw Simon and Andrew the brother of Simon casting a net in the sea; for they were fishermen. And Jesus said to them, 'Follow me and I will make you become fishers of men.' And immediately they left their nets and followed him. And going on a little further, he saw James the son of Zebedee and John his brother, who were in their boat mending the nets. And immediately he called them; and they left their father Zebedee in the boat with the hired servants, and followed him (Mark 1.16–20).

Mark does nothing to explain the psychology of the story; he says nothing about what the men were waiting for; or what they thought about Jesus at this time; or what they expected Jesus to give them. Mark is not writing a psychological study of the Twelve, or of Jesus, but theology in dramatic form.

The gospel is proclaimed by Jesus to two pairs of brothers, and it comes to them as an invitation – 'he called them'; they accept the invitation, and the proof that they have accepted it is that they leave what they were doing and follow Jesus instead.

The original readers of Mark's gospel would not need any account of what was going on in the minds of the four fishermen at the time of their call, and it would not have been relevant had Mark been in a position to provide it, which he probably was not. Those who first read Mark had done the same thing themselves; they had heard the gospel preached in Rome or wherever they were, and they had believed and joined the followers of Jesus. Mark's readers would understand the fishermen, because they knew themselves. So if we are to understand the gospel in the same way we must find a similar pattern of response within our own situation.

The first time that we hear the challenge of the gospel, it will demand that we look afresh at some particular aspect of our living. A man may be confronted with the new thinking of Jesus at some turning point in his career. The natural advantages of status, pay or career prospects may be in opposition to some deeply recognized principle. At that moment of choice 'faith' will be expressed or denied by the practical decision.

Such a crisis can be the occasion to which a person looks back as his Damascus road; the moment when he first recognized clearly the presence of Jesus within a situation and heard the call to which he then became a witness. The dramatic disclosure of one particular occasion is not the only way that a shift occurs. More often it may be that in reflection on the past we are brought up against the recognition that what we were doing was in fact far different from the gospel we imagined that we served. A different kind of recognition dawns as we realize that we are called and recalled even within the context of our apparent dedication to God's cause.

Rather than producing an imaginary example, let one of the authors put this in terms of his own experience.

When Christian Aid was a new thing, I was a keen young incumbent who wanted to promote its cause in the town. I was advised that what was needed was a public meeting at which the mayor would preside and to which the local notables including church leaders could be invited. The result was an event of which the press took due note; committees were formed and the project proceeded very satisfactorily.

Valuable results were achieved in terms of local participation in a fund-raising effort, which had an explicitly Christian cause in view. Yet on reflection it emerged that by setting the campaign up in this way some people were pushed into participation by social pressures, a desire to be doing the 'in thing' or an inability to refuse a request. The mixed motives resulted later in moments of bitterness and disagreement as participants felt themselves being asked to do more than they had bargained for or were not adequately thanked for such efforts as they had made.

As I promoted the work for Christian Aid I was behaving as a white middle-class liberal, which after all is what I am, and doubtless there is a place for them in the kingdom! What I began had about it a potentiality for becoming an expression of the gospel. Perhaps for some people it was indeed that, as they gave or worked or cared. In retrospect, I think that for myself it was a good job reasonably well done, paying certain dividends in enhanced self-esteem and a quiet satisfaction that the church I represented was appearing in a favourable light to a majority of the public. But I can recognize that my commitment was a limited one: I was concerned to plead a cause that involved only a moderate charitable support of those in need. The appeal was carefully expressed in acceptable terms. I had not penetrated to what I now believe is the ultimate demand of the gospel, to think afresh about possessions and to ask uncomfortable political questions concerning the economic structures which keep nations poor. Such thoughts do not make a secure platform from which to appeal to the general public for support. It is not the stuff for popular speeches at fund-raising events. I am not sure that the mayor would have liked it.

To realize this dilemma is to feel the excess and impracticality of the gospel. Yet something needs to be done. Hunger cries out to be satisfied; the work of Christian Aid demands support. I cannot wait to act until an ideal attitude has been achieved by others or even by myself. I have humbly to recognize the ambivalence of my situation and the limitations which it places on me. I am not loving enough: I do not care with all my heart. Yet the gospel lays on me the necessity grounded in love, to discover that which I can realistically do and to channel my uncomfortable excessive awareness of inadequacy into accomplishing that limited objective. One other consequence ensues. This deprives me of any glow of self-satisfaction. I am not a splendid benefactor but an unprofitable servant. As well as acting, I must be prepared to stand up and be counted when the cause is challenged. Only I must be careful that it is in the end Christ to whom any allegiance is given and not some particular course of action. If I am the partisan supporter of this or that cause, then I shall be tempted to ride roughshod over my opponents. As Christ's man I must be prepared to recognize him not only in the remote African whom I want to benefit, but in the local churchman who attacks my theology and impugns my motives!

The gospel as I hear it witnesses to me about God's way and not my own. As I respond to it I bear witness that what I have heard is true and others from this may receive the testimony which challenges them to the response of faith.

If this double process is to happen we must have some certainty that we are thinking in the gospel way; as St Paul put it, that we have 'the mind of Christ', that his presence is with us. For this some objective criteria are needed. This seems to have been the reason why the gospels were written, and the way in which the stories in them were remembered and passed on. The Christians met each week for the eucharist, to break bread together in obedience to the command of Jesus (Luke 22.19; I Cor. 11.24). At the beginning of the meeting, somebody told a story about Jesus in the days of his flesh: how he healed a sick person; argued with the Jews about God and his ways; com-

41

manded his disciples to live in view of the coming kingdom of God. But these were not simply historical reminiscences; they were not recalling a dead man's words and actions. Nor were they talking and thinking about one who was absent from them. The pre-supposition on which they met was that Jesus was alive and well and with them. Matthew put this as the last line in his book, and he meant it to be the key to the understanding of it all: 'I am with you always, to the close of the age' (Matt. 28.30; see also 1.23; 10.40; 18.5, 20; 23.8, 10; 25.31–46).

The point of telling stories about Jesus at the eucharist, and later of writing gospels to be read at the eucharist, was to focus attention on the Lord whom they believed to be present to do the same things as those that he had done in the days of his flesh: to make men whole; to declare the ways of God; and to enable the disciples to do God's will. Gospel stories are stories about the Lord and his disciples; and faith is faith in the Lord who is present with his disciples, declaring to them again and again, 'Your faith has made you well' (Mark 5.34; 10.52).

So the testimony to Christ is declared in the gospel stories but he is also present in the lives and decisions of all those who have been his witnesses in the succeeding generations.

The church today is called to continue that witness. Just as the first century Christians read the story of the apostles' call and recognized themselves, so each generation in its own way authenticates the New Testament experience. They can say to their contemporaries, 'We too have seen and known . . .' At the same time it is by the New Testament that they check their vision so that it remains true to the gospel tradition because it is the same Lord who calls the continuing succession of witnesses that the world may believe.

8 · Invitation and Possibility

We have written of the gospel as 'invitation' and 'challenge'. Just how compelling do we find its claims to be? There is the haunting comment of the Lancashireman to an acquaintance: 'You're a churchwarden are 'ee? Now my 'obby's breeding pigeons.' Most people would not have put it as blatantly as that, but in general there is the impression that the affairs of the gospel are for those who are interested in that kind of thing: very much an optional extra.

This is far from the way in which the New Testament sees its priorities. Even the idea of an invitation may weaken the impression of urgency. After all there is nothing discreditable about refusing an invitation; you simply say that you regret you cannot come because of a previous engagement. No one is under an obligation to accept all the invitations he receives; in some areas and jobs it would be physically impossible to do so. The gospel is not like that.

In Matthew's version of the parable of the invitations to the wedding, the one who is sending out the invitations is a king (Matt. 22.2); an invitation from a king is a command. In the story of the call of the disciples, the words of Jesus to Simon and Andrew are 'Follow me', not our polite 'The pleasure of your company is requested'. Perhaps we should say, therefore, that the gospel produces faith, not by inviting it, but by commanding it. An invitation or call from God is a command, with no space for RSVP. This aspect of the gospel is seen in another parable in Matthew:

'What do you think? A man had two sons; and he went to the first and said, "Son, go and work in the vineyard today," and he answered "I will not"; but afterward he repented and went. And he went to the second and said the same; and he answered "I go, sir," but did not go. Which of the two did the will of his father?' They said, 'The first.' Jesus said to them, 'Truly, I say to you, the tax collectors and the harlots go into the kingdom of God before you. For John came to you in the way of righteousness, and you did not believe him, but the tax collectors and the harlots believed him; and even when you saw it, you did not afterward repent and believe him' (Matt. 21.28–32).

Repent (a differnt word in Greek from Mark 1.15, but it likewise means to change one's mind) and believe is the twofold response to the gospel; and the gospel is expressed here in the form of a command: 'Go and work in the vineyard today.' Invitation is too weak a word to describe the gospel adequately. The man who hears the gospel would not say that what comes to him is like an invitation to an occasion of some kind; he would be much more likely to say that it has the force of a command which he should not dare to disobey. In order to see why the gospel is a command, we shall have to return to Mark.

At the beginning of his book, Mark spoke in a general way of faith in the gospel (1.15) and following Jesus (1.17f, 20; 2.14, 15); it is only in the second part of the book that he begins to explain what following Jesus means – that is to say, what is involved in believing in the gospel.

If any man would come after me, let him deny himself and take up his cross and follow me. For whoever would save his life will lose it; and whoever loses his life for my sake and the gospel's will save it (Mark 8.34ff.).

When the gospel is preached, the hearer is presented with the alternatives, faith or unbelief; one way leads to salvation, and the other to destruction. The gospel places the hearer in a position in which he must decide between life and death, and commands him to choose life, but at the cost of his death. The faith for which the gospel calls is therefore unlimited faith, because it is to be maintained up to the believer's destruction. The gospel, therefore, deals with ultimate matters, not choices that have no lasting importance. It is the gospel of God (Mark 1.14) and it is God who saves and destroys.

How is it possible to say that God destroys, if he loves? At least we must say that the gospel commands us to live in accordance with the way things really are which includes catastrophe and loss; it recalls us from the false hopes and ambitions that we have proposed for ourselves, and tells us that these are dead ends, with no future in that direction; if we identify ourselves with them we are wasting our lives, and our plans will never mature.

The gospel is a command from God to leave behind a life that is doomed to destruction, and risk everything for a different kind of living, which is called faith, and to which is attached the promise of salvation, because it is in accordance with the way things really are.

We have seen that the gospel is an invitation to believe, and a command to believe (since it is a matter of life and death); what we must see now is that it enables faith. It opens up the possibility of a new life, an alternative way of living, in an alternative society. It says, Come out of the world and live in the church; separate yourself from the old way of life and live the new life which is faith. In this new life, what was impossible before is now made possible, because 'All things are possible to him who believes' (Mark 9.23).

The gospel is therefore a message about yourself, telling you that you can do things you had thought you could not do, just as one might say to a person learning to swim or ride a bicycle, Now you can do it. The gospel says, Now you can do everything – that is, everything that God wills.

But in what sense does the gospel enable faith? The kind of things that Jesus was saying may seem quite impossible when we try to spell them out in cold print. The disciples found that they could take devastating practical risks like leaving their jobs, defying the Jewish authorities, going out into the world under the threat of persecution. At first such things were possible because Jesus himself was with them. Later they were convinced of his risen presence in a different mode, but no less certainly among them.

Can we still point to the same enabling power at work within the Christian community today? Without it the kind of insights we have been pursuing become paradoxical nonsense. Only a group of people who are convinced that in some way God will give what he commands, can take the gospel seriously. In any other circumstances it could only be an invitation to despair.

The life of the Christian community must necessarily be the vehicle through which the sustaining power is communicated. Yet throughout its history the church has only partially succeeded in performing this task. The ideal continually reappears only to be submerged in practice. The gospel, however clearly seen, is quickly imprisoned in the formal structures beloved by institutions. But structures are not wantonly developed for their own sake. They represent one way of holding chaos at bay.

Since the gospel is concerned with people in relationship to one another and to God, any embodiment of it must make provision for the needs of those who come together. One way of doing this is to provide rules and to set standards. The result is that people, as they say, 'Know where they are'. But that can stop them developing, although it may have the advantage of allaying anxiety. This was the quarrel that Jesus had with the religious system of his day. His objective was to set men free and not to maintain a particular 'church'. The Jews, however, had come to equate the system with the service of God, and so could not believe that he was to be found. outside it. When Jesus seemed to be offering a free relationship of forgiveness to all men, and not simply for those who had in some way earned it by obedience to the system, he appeared as an enemy of God.

In this and in many other ways, Jesus failed to conform to popular expectations. In the eyes of the Establishment he was not recognizable as a prophet: they could dismiss him as 'a glutton and a drunkard, a friend of tax collectors and sinners' (Matt. 11.19). When expectations are not fulfilled people become angry. Part of the scandal of the gospel is that it always confounds the reasonable expectations of the prudent man. It either exceeds them or turns them upside down. If people are to survive the predictable opposition, which will arise as they attempt to give expression to this paradox, they must have some kind of support system which enables them to stay open to its creative pattern. The life of faith is not possible without the community of faith. What form that must take is part of the Christian exploration in each generation.

9 · Free for All

'I've ceased to matter.' 'Nobody cares.' The complaint is seldom articulated in just those terms, but recognized or not it can lie behind a wide range of human behaviour. The wife who has an affair; the teenager who takes to pilfering; the patient who attempts suicide and the business man who drives on frantically towards his coronary are in their various ways proving something about themselves that in another frame of reference is being denied. 'I am significant,' the wife is saying, and it may not be her husband that she needs to convince but her own inner doubts. So, too, the younger person is stating something about his own value. A sense of badness, 'the world would be better without me,' underlies many attempts at suicide. It can be another side of the same coin that pushes a man to overwork so that he can keep the inner accusation at bay with the answer 'Look, I *am* some use; here are the things I've done to prove it.'

The more one thinks about it, the more one realizes that a great deal of human living and not just deviant behaviour is concerned with proving the thesis 'I'm OK.' Certainly the opposite assumption of inner worthlessness is one of the root causes of mental illness. So it should come as good news to people that this is not God's estimate of us. As a loving father he approaches us with a gift, not with a bribe nor a reward but with a present. As parents we use what we give as a way of ensuring future conformity – 'All right, you can watch the Saturday film if you go straight to bed afterwards' – or as recognition of actions – 'Now that you've got your A levels I'll pay for driving lessons.' Can we really think that God's actions are so different from our own?

The Bible is most insistent upon the central notion of 'grace' in God's approach to us.

A reward is not a present, because a reward is earned, but a present is not. A reward is payment for work that has been done, and it is due; it is owed, because it has been earned. A reward is payment for work that was done in the past. The point is made by Paul: 'To one who works, his wages are not reckoned as a gift but as his due' (Rom. 4.4). Similarly, a bribe is not a present, because a bribe is payment for work which is expected in the future; a bribe is a pre-payment. The person who receives a bribe owes the work, and the work is due subsequently.

Rewards and bribes have to do with work, in the past or in the future. But a present has nothing to do with work, and it has no reference to past or future. A present is related to the moment in which it is given, and it looks neither backwards nor forwards. The same point could be made by saying that rewards and bribes imply a contract between two parties; gifts do not. Gifts express love; the giver of gifts is neither rewarding nor bribing; he is not establishing a contract that involves work; and the receiver of gifts is not put under contract to the giver. The relationship between a giver and a receiver is one of love. And this is what John's gospel says of Christ's coming: 'God so loved the world that he gave . . .' (John 3.16).

Maybe there is still a doubt in our minds. Do gifts always come unexpectedly, out of the blue? Do not people say, 'I am expecting a present today'? Is it not possible to ask for presents? It certainly is possible to ask for them, but the asking does not tie the giver to giving them; he remains free, to give or not to give. The more certainly a present is expected, the less it is a present. The one exception to this might be the case when the receiver is sure of the attitude of love on the part of the giver; then it is really the attitude he is certain about, and not the gift that expresses the attitude. Givers of presents are free; there cannot be an obligation to give. If there were an obligation, then the 'presents' would in fact be either rewards or bribes. (Or perhaps we should say that the obligation to give is of a different kind from the obligation to pay; the latter is the result of an agreement, the former is unilateral and self-imposed.)

But do we really want God to behave like this? Let us go back to our hard-working business man who has built up his own firm in the teeth of bitter competition. Now in his early fifties, he is beginning to recognize the cost in terms of his marriage and his health. Let us ask him to comment on a story from Matthew: 'The kingdom of heaven is like treasure hidden in a field, which a man found and covered up; then in his joy he goes and sells all that he has and buys that field' (Matt. 13.44). Perhaps we can unpack the familiar account in words which he appreciates.

The joy of coming across the treasure was so great that it enabled the man to do whatever was necessary to buy the field; that is, to sell all that he had, without any regrets. 'Sell all that you have' sounds terrifying: 'all' includes the objects that are so familiar, and make one feel secure. But this was not how it was for the man in the parable. For one thing, he was so poor that the capital value of his possessions was only equal to the price of a field; he had not much to lose. But in any case, he was on to a dead certainty; he was simply realizing his capital temporarily, in order to use it more profitably. Suppose his goods were worth £500; and that that was the price of the field. He sells his goods, is paid the £500, buys the field for the £500, and then digs up the treasure. He can now resell the field and recover the £500. It may be that he will actually sell it at a profit: the value of the land will have been increased when it is known that it had treasure in it. Somebody will speculate on there being still more hidden away in it. When this is done he can buy back his goods. In the end, he has all his personal effects, and the treasure. He has lost nothing; it is an 'absolute gift'.

How would our business friend react? With an envious chuckle: 'Lucky fellow: I wish I'd had a break like that'? Or might there be some sense of unfairness, a demand that life should be about rewards and deserts – not about getting things free?

This was in fact the fundamental point of disagreement between Jesus and the Pharisees. They built their claim to God's favour upon being faithful, even meticulous observers of the Law. Jesus shocked them by spending his time with those whose lives merited no approval, the publicans and sinners. The point was made but so revolutionary was it that it was not taken.

It is an absolutely fundamental truth. No one can be in receipt of the gospel who is trying to justify himself. The fact that he is trying to justify himself proves that he has not yet heard the gospel, or that if he has heard it he has forgotten what he has heard. It is impossible to be at one and the same time a believer in the justification which God gives through faith in Christ, and one who seeks his own justification by works. To try to be right with God by works is to nullify the grace of God; it is to try to pay for what is in fact a present, and therefore to destroy its quality as a gift.

To receive the gospel of the grace of God is to accept righteousness as a present from God. But no one can have righteousness as a present, and be simultaneously trying to earn it. Paul's own words are:

> If any other man thinks he has reason for confidence in the flesh, I have more: circumcised on the eighth day, of the people of Israel, of the tribe of Benjamin, a Hebrew born of Hebrews; as to the law a Pharisee, as to zeal a persecutor of the church, as to righteousness under the law blameless. But whatever gain I had, I counted as loss for the sake of Christ. Indeed I count everything as loss because of the surpassing worth of knowing Christ Jesus my Lord. For his sake I have suffered the loss of all things, and count them as refuse, in order that I may gain Christ and be found in him, not having a righteousness of my own, based on law, but that which is through faith in Christ, the righteousness from God that depends on faith (Phil. 3.4–9).

The background to this passage, and to all the talk of justification by faith or by works, is a controversy among Christians in the forties and fifties of the first century. The question at issue was whether disciples of Christ had to keep the Jewish law or not. It was debated in a particularly acute and bitter manner in those churches where the majority of members were Gentile rather than Jewish; that is, in the churches founded by Paul, the apostle to the Gentiles. Moreover, it seems that people travelled from one church to another in order to 'correct' what they regarded as the errors of those who had been converted by Paul. We hear of this matter in Galatia, in Corinth, and in Rome where Paul's opponents appear to have arrived ahead of him, hence his letter to the Romans. What they said was, 'You must do the things that are laid down in the law, such as circumcision, the sacred calendar of feasts and fasts, and the regulations about food. The gospel by itself is not enough; faith by itself is not enough. You must have both the law and the gospel, in order to be right with God, and have his favour and his peace'. They were the first people to live by the slogan, beloved of the English, 'It is not a question of either/or, but of both/and.'

For Paul the issue is clear cut: either a righteousness of one's own, or the righteousness from God; either works, or grace; either wages, or gift. And if the choice is made for righteousness from God's grace as a gift, then every attempt to justify oneself by doing works that earn wages must be given up. The life of faith is a continual acceptance of the gift of righteousness. We return again and again to the love of God which is there before we do anything; we return to God who is always for us. This returning demands faith, because it involves disregarding part of the evidence, and attending solely to another part. What has to be disregarded is the evidence of one's own sin. What has to be attended to is the love of God, which is made known by the death of Christ.

If this is the central truth of the gospel, the good news that sets people free from the endless struggle to achieve their worth, then it must find expression wherever Christians come together. It is the purpose of the two sacraments of the gospel to declare this in such a way that it moves from an interesting idea into a saving truth that touches a person's life at its depths.

Both emphasize the element of gift in God's relationship with man. The images which express the meaning of baptism are of new birth and the invasion of power like wind and fire. You cannot arrange to be born or qualify for the privilege. All you can do is to receive what is given.

In the same way the act of feeding, which is the central image of eucharistic worship, depends on the initiative of the giver. The guests have nothing to contribute except to ensure that they are there.

To remind themselves of this, the first Christians told the stories of Jesus eating with the tax gatherers and the shady characters and presumably gratefully identified themselves with such company. The difficulty comes when the church has to fulfil the double role, of host as well as guest. The institution issues the invitations in the Lord's name and seems to find it difficult to share his catholic taste in company! It is at this point that church practice and discipline tend to part company with the gospel. How the tension can be held must be the next stage in our enquiry.

10 · Presence and Reality

Baptism and communion are the two almost universal expressions of life through the gospel. The question we have to ask is whether as they are now celebrated these sacraments adequately declare the truths which they are meant to embody. The response to the enquiry of those who heard Peter's Pentecost sermon was 'Repent, and be baptized every one of you' (Acts 2.38). We have looked carefully at the meaning of repentance and found it demands a radical change of attitude. A whole set of assumptions needs to be changed: this ties up with the image of a totally new birth or a drowning into life.

The change envisaged is total, but it comes not through the superhuman efforts of the person concerned but as the gift of God. Birth is the one event in your life which you cannot arrange for yourself, which is why the language of new birth is appropriate for the beginning of life in the gospel. The same is true of resurrection from the dead. Again the person is in the position of total helplessness; it is only help coming from outside which can bring new life.

So baptism is the sacrament of God's sovereign activity and generosity. It is the gift of living water bringing to the barren ground what it cannot in itself possess.

This is how we must speak if we look objectively at the act of baptism. From within perhaps it will feel to be different – at least when the act of initiation is done at a time when the recipient can feel at all. The offer which is made will not seem to be an easy option.

The long human history of unloving relationships has left its mark on the whole race. We do not naturally open ourselves out to love and be loved. So we find we have to approach this gift of God through a difficult torrent that unselfs us, washing away, perhaps drowning away, the defences of our fear-ridden natures; just as the man had to sell everything he had, to buy the field where the treasure was. Looked at from this point of view the demand to give up certain attitudes is the most obvious part of the process. Yet even then, the surrender made, the new Christian reports his experience as new birth, the opening out of the gift of life. He has not lost himself, he is found.

Let us be quite clear that the old system of bribes and rewards has not crept in by the back door. Baptism does demand a 'death', a letting go of old attitudes but this, which is repentance and faith, is not a payment. The new life is not purchased by a change of mind or by trust in God and obedience to him. Bribes and rewards refer to the future or the past, gifts are about now. So too is the gospel. It does not say 'You will be God's son if you do something to earn it.' Nor is it 'You are God's son because you did something in the past.' The gospel is 'You are God's son, now.'

That is the theological truth. Is it reflected in church practice?

An institution wants to protect its membership from undesirable adherents. Obviously, this is in its own interests: a well-run club likes to be sure that a member can leave his coat without fear of losing his wallet. It could be also claimed that anything less than this would be bad for public relations. Who would want to join an association of known deviants – like quislings and sinners and whores? So the institution builds its walls high to keep out undesirables and those who gain admission are under some pressure to maintain the facade of their respectability.

This very natural human attitude is sometimes given liturgical expression in extravagant demands about the renunciation of evil before a person is initiated. Almost always in both baptism and eucharist the balance tips from 'gift' to 'demand' as the local congregation gives expression to its feelings or the wider church draws up its 'rules of membership'.

Of course repentance goes with baptism and if we think of that in terms of giving up the past then we may say 'Until you are properly sorry you are not fit to be baptized.' But that is to invert the pattern of the New Testament. It is because Jesus has gone to the house of Zacchaeus that the tax-gatherer sees life from a different point of view and makes his renunciation (Luke

19.8–10). The coming of Christ to his house is not conditional upon certain steps being taken.

So baptism must be the act of the church in God's name, following his pattern of generosity. But if it is not to become an empty gesture, there must be commitment by the believing community towards the person received, whether infant or adult. Provision must be made for an effective expression of love. This will include a sustained interest in the persons baptized throughout their period of growth in the faith, and the provision of the kind of community in which the way of renewed repentance is possible.

This kind of development will lead on to the experience of the communicant life.

The element of demand rather than gift quickly takes over here too. Confirmation candidates are taught about 'their duty to attend the eucharist', as though it might be something that in normal circumstances they would be inclined to avoid. Essentially the eucharist should be experienced as a place of feeding; the images are the picnic in Galilee with thousands fed, the participation in God's gift of freedom from Egypt, the banquet of the returning victor. Someone invited to participate might expect to be welcomed and would be sure that he was wanted for himself. It is, after all, only the very worst kind of wedding where one suspects that the invitation was sent either because it would have been too embarrassing to miss one out, or because it was hoped that it would ensure a handsome present for the bride and groom.

If instead of the sense of duty there is to be the atmosphere of welcome that draws people irresistibly to the sharing of worship, what ingredients must it contain? First there must be an opportunity for intimate meeting. At the level of human feeling this is the only way in which a person can know that he is given value in himself as a reflection of God's love for him.

When members have come into some rapport with one another they will then be ready to turn to the second element, the sacramental participation by bread and wine in the whole truth of the gospel, summed up in the cross and resurrection. Here each individual opens his life out to accept the pattern of losing and finding. It is by receiving God's Spirit into ourselves that we are enabled to love our children unselfishly, to resist the

54

pressures of ambition or live in all the other ways for others. This is to be aware of the presence of God and the possibility of being overshadowed by him.

These seem to be the two necessary ingredients for an authentic gospel event to occur. They represent the taking seriously of both the human presences and the divine presence. A congregation needs to take its role as 'host' sufficiently seriously to make the necessary provision for this to occur.

In practice the first of these two elements of the eucharist which involves the recognition and the giving value to each participant is, for the most part, missing in the formal worship of the churches. Instead, to sit down in many congregations is to be submerged in a dependent group dominated by the clerical officiant. This is precisely the opposite of what is required. A worshipper can actually be diminished by participation in such a liturgy. And such an experience is a direct contradiction of the gospel.

Let us try to imagine what all this might mean in practical terms. Forgetting 'church' as we at present know it, suppose the pattern of Sunday worship were for twelve people to come together in a house. The natural thing would be to arrive and to drink a cup of coffee. At this point, since the majority would know each other well through regular contact, there would be an opportunity for hearing about the events of the week, what had gone well, who was in trouble, what difficulties had arisen. If there were strangers they could be welcomed and something discovered about them, so that they felt they had an identity within the group.

When sufficient exchange had taken place, the authorized president would call the meeting to order, perhaps with a formal greeting. The liturgy of the Word would doubtless have some fixed elements related to the Christian year, so that the group was aware of its membership of a much larger organization stretching, not only horizontally in geography, but backwards in time. Within the intimacy of this kind of church the gifts and weaknesses of each member would be known and capable of acknowledgment. Therefore it would not be left to one voice to expound the scriptures. All from their various standpoints might be expected to contribute to an understanding.

So while it had its roots in the past, the focus of group

awareness would be the present. First of all they would need to be aware of one another, sensitive to the unexpressed needs. The intercessions might be the place where this corporate support was given the clearest expression. It would not, however, be confined to words. A hand stretched out may express more than a careful phrase. At the time of the confession one person might find it right to turn silently to another and make some gesture of penitence or forgiveness. Once the members had found their own needs met, their ability to care for others should expand to include the wider concerns of the church and the world.

Part of the meaning of meeting in the context of the eucharist also includes a recognition of the shared life of the church throughout the ages. An Orthodox priest in a tiny country church may well claim to have had last Sunday a congregation of thousands. He will not be suffering from the Western obsession with success which makes clergy exaggerate their communicant figures. He will merely be confidently affirming his sense of participation in the unending worship of the church. But these added dimensions seem to spring most naturally out of the experience of a common life which gives to each individual his place, recognizing the uniqueness of his contribution in the body of Christ. So the present awareness of the participants need not obscure the wider context of the eucharist. In fact, ideally it should enhance it.

If such were the norm for weekly worship, there would be another aspect of worship to be expressed in a periodic gathering together of all the small congregations into a dramatic assembly where an emphasis was placed on the approach to the majesty of God.

There are two modes of worship. In the one, each person should have the opportunity to express something of himself; in the other, he must be taken out of himself.

Much else could be written in detail about possible expressions of the gospel in liturgical life, but in the end each congregation must find its own appropriate patterns. If part of the present need is to break out of stereotyped ways of worship, this process will not be helped by urging new stereotypes upon people. The essence of Christian worship is not the following of a ritual but the free response of God's people to his presence. In this sense as every human encounter is a fresh occasion, so each eucharist needs to have about it a spontaneity which retains the freshness even though regular patterns of worship come to be adopted. What is essential is that at the heart of all meeting, the eucharistic exchange shall bring each participant to a sense of his own value before God. Out of this certainty grow the peace and the love which the world can recognize as the presence of God's Spirit.

11 · Games and Grace

When children first learn to play a game they have a very special attitude about the rules. The pattern was carefully observed by Piaget, the famous educational psychologist. He took the example of children learning to play marbles. Three stages emerged. First the very young ones just enjoyed the marbles as toys, doing whatever they wanted with them. From the age of five to nine the idea of 'the rules' took over. During this period Piaget says 'the rules are regarded as sacred and inviolable, emanating from adults and lasting for ever'. The children have a feeling that unless they are followed exactly something is wrong and the proper game is not being played.

It is only later that they are able to understand an adult approach which sees the rules as being a means of facilitating the play which is desired and therefore capable of modification at the will of the players. When you first begin, the rules are the game, because that is the way you have learnt it. To discover that there is a game which matters more is a later development. What Piaget understood from the game of marbles seems to shed light on a lot of behaviour way beyond the playground or the classroom.

All through life there are occasions when people confuse the method of doing something with the thing in itself. In the kitchen there are anxious cooks who slavishly follow a recipe and resist any modification. In contrast there are others who give their intuition full rein, blithely dropping whatever is handy into the saucepan and yet producing a delicious result. In the domestic field the harsh reality of needing to produce a meal whatever ingredients are available may persuade the rigid cook to sit more lightly to the instructions. Yet there may still be a feeling that if some ingredient is missing, however acceptable the

58

result may be, it is not *proper* Shepherd's Pie. In the medical profession, too, the way of doing things can become paramount. Wearing the right clothes, or the act of giving a prescription, or even the bedside manner, can be mistaken for the art of healing. The one sphere where method and purpose seem to get most inextricably confused is that of religious ritual.

The child in all of us believes in magic. Magic is about power achieved through ritual. The words must be exactly right and said in the prescribed conditions; only so will the spell or the incantation work. The real evil of magic is not that it is used for harmful purposes, so that you can distinguish black from white magic, but that it starts from the assumption that ritual gives power. The person with the secret dances the rain dance, chants the spell, mumbles the curse or whatever it may be and from this power proceeds. Part of the magical belief is that spirits or powers are commanded by these processes.

The world of the gospel is the complete opposite of the magical search for power. There is not a God who has to be either persuaded, enticed or entrapped to do our bidding. He is entirely free and at the same time entirely for us. The spell of the magician is designed to summon 'spirits from the vasty deep'. God in Jesus says 'Lo, I am with you always, to the close of the age' (Matt. 28.20). There is no point in weaving spells to conjure power when God has said 'ask and you shall receive'.

Somehow this seems all too surprising for our human minds to accept. Surely God could not be all that accessible? If he were, would people still respect him? After all, there is the old proverb 'Familiarity breeds contempt' and worldly rulers have found a great advantage in a little bit of mystique to keep their subjects in awe of them.

The religious traditions of mankind have no doubt at all that the gods need to be approached with care. Amongst these the Jewish law set up a careful code of ritual washings and purificatory sacrifices. The approach to God was most safely made through designated persons who had about them a particular quality though even these needed specialized protective clothing for the encounter.

Because of the uncertainty about God and the attitudes he might have, a great emphasis was laid upon the rules of the approach. This was the only contribution that man could make to the encounter so it must be done absolutely right. This is what most of the book of Leviticus is dedicated to ensuring should happen. All this is part of human thinking about God which we saw earlier in chapter 3. It finds itself turned round through 180° when it meets the gospel.

The scandal of Jesus was that he cut all the rules down to size. He was not a person who tore them up. He allowed them their place as guidelines but all that he said and did was designed to make it clear that the ultimate purpose of the religious system was the free encounter of man with God, at which point the 'system' is transcended. Where the rules helped prepare the way, they were to be followed and where they became an obstacle they must be set aside.

The reaction of the Pharisees and the religious men of his day was precisely that of children who had not yet learned to distinguish between the rules and the game. They argued that if you healed on the Sabbath, ate with unwashed hands or allowed a ritually unclean woman to touch you, you could not possibly be a holy man. For such people it was an unbearable paradox that when God's law took flesh in a human being he was able to go behind the written words in which the law had previously been formalized.

As Christians we are quick to condemn the Pharisees. We see through their mistakes in the pages of the New Testament. We find it more difficult to understand that we ourselves are often caught in the same trap. There have been times when volumes of Christian theology have poured from the presses arguing about the conditions which constitute a 'valid eucharist'. This presumably was intended to define the kind of occasion when you could be sure that the Lord was present in the celebration of the sacrament. The sort of conditions which from time to time have been thought necessary have included the right sort of bread, fermented wine (grape juice will not do), a minister bearing the authority of a particular kind of ordination, a duly consecrated stone altar and so on. The good Scottish Episcopalian chaplain in 1745 who celebrated the holy communion with oat cakes and whisky before battle had no such careful respect for rules – but how many devout Christians would have condemned his licence in the matter?

If the gospel sets us free from the rigid approach of a law-bound spirituality, what sort of prayer does it make possible? If we remember the children with their marbles we will not be led into the mistake of thinking that no pattern or discipline is required at all. The first acquaintance with a new vision might lead to a brief period of euphoria when it was felt that 'anything goes'. As quickly as when the delighted infants start throwing their new toys into the air, it becomes apparent that order is necessary! But the church often seems so afraid of anarchy that it has given the impression that discipline *is* the spiritual life.

When it comes to prayers perhaps the best-known saying in the New Testament is 'Ask, and it will be given you' (Matt. 7.7). The uninhibited expression of need is declared to be the basic ingredient. All the careful preparatory business of sacrifice which fills the Old Testament is swept away. Once the imagery had been that of humble petitioners in the court of a great king; now the barriers are down and the children are told to approach their father on the assumption that he is already on their side.

Along with the ease in asking, the first Christians emphasized the frequency of thanksgiving. Because the basic element in their relationship with God was love, their mood was bound to reflect delight and enjoyment.

The gospel pattern seems so obvious and so natural. We might wonder how Christian believers ever fell away from it. Or at least we might, until we paused to recognize how quickly we turn the life of grace back into a game with rules.

There may be a time when for the individual or a small group, prayer has taken on a new dimension. It feels as though the heavens are open; there is a sense of the presence with them. 'That's right,' they say, 'that's how it ought to be.' The result is that they begin to try to reproduce the circumstances in which the disclosure occurred, and to make them into rules for how prayer *must* happen. There is no more rigid liturgical strait-jacket than the stereo-typed phrases that are trotted out at supposedly extempore prayer meetings, or any other act of worship which tries to recapture a former experience of grace.

Here is a fundamental distinction. Any authentic encounter is of its nature unique, whether between person and person, or between man and God. Games can be repeated at will. So we can say 'Tomorrow we will play football.' But if a person says 'Tomorrow I will fall in love' we reply 'You are not serious; love isn't like that. You are treating it as a game.' So were we wrong in drawing a parallel between Piaget's observations of children playing marbles and the patterns of religious behaviour? Were we confusing the world of games and the world of real life?

For children the growing up process is largely achieved through experimenting with various roles. They play at mothers and fathers; later they will be adult and then parenthood is no game. Adolescents try out various roles, including that of personal commitment but they are not yet ready for it. Fiction in the form of novels, TV plays or films stimulates the imagination to new possibilities. If a person tries them out they will remain games until they become authentic parts of that individual's self-expression. Then they will come from within and will in no sense be played according to an external set of rules.

Here is a clue to the distinction which is made between fasting under the old covenant and under the new. The Pharisees and John's disciples fasted according to the rule book; the disciples of Jesus were observed not to fast and this gave rise to a question 'why not?'. The reply is given that they will fast when they have cause for it.

> Can the wedding guests fast while the bridegroom is with them? As long as they have the bridegroom with them, they cannot fast. The days will come, when the bridegroom is taken away from them, and then they will fast in that day (Mark 2.19, 20).

This is the difference between a ritual observance of fish on Fridays and the attendance at an Oxfam bread and cheese lunch because a person believes that the needs of the starving demand this expression of self-denial. One represents the keeping of a set of rules, the other is the authentic response of Christian obedience. The border line between the two is something which can only be determined by the individual himself. It is he who must distinguish between the religious 'game', tough and costly as it may be, designed to make him into something by the training that he has undertaken, and the stirring of grace within him which produces the fruit of the Spirit.

This is what the gospel way of prayer is all about. It is not a process of self-culture, but a personal response to the encounter with love. So we tell our needs openly; we express our distress in fasting: We are grateful, we may also be angry or resentful and we say so. As we take seriously the promise of God's presence we will not have to be reminded to do all this as part of our spiritual discipline; we will be responding in these ways because that is how the situation is.

Prayer as response is the opposite to prayer as discipline. This is a mode which at the present Christians seem to be discovering, largely out of renewed contacts with the spirituality of the East. It starts with a willingness to be open to what is. This is in marked contrast to the Western habit of trying to rearrange things in order to improve them. When we achieve the stillness of a reflecting pool we allow God to invade us through other people, through his created world or through situations. We perceive them as they are instead of imposing our interpretation upon them. And this is the beginning of contemplative prayer: for by experiencing the being of the other, we discover the possibility of praise. We cease to be the centre of our world, ordering it neatly round us to suit ourselves or to fit our prearranged understanding of it. By allowing things to approach us as themselves and losing our tight control over them, we enter into the inheritance of a far richer world. The things and the persons so perceived lead us into the depths of God.

Such prayer is not a steady discipline to which we must be urged. It is an experience of vision to which we will want to return again and again. But there are no rules to make it happen; a loving attentiveness to what is brings us into a fresh contact with God who lies at the heart of all that he has made and sustains in being.

In much advice that is given to Christians about prayer, particularly in confirmation manuals, the emphasis is over and over again on duty and serious-minded application. When a person is presented with something that is genuinely new, exciting, joyful and love-promoting, he does not need stern reminders of his obligation to become involved: he wants the good thing he has recognized.

We need to ask ourselves whether the way that we·pray or encourage others to do so squares with the kind of claims that are made for the gospel. If not, then are we praying as Christians or as pagans hopefully searching after a God we do not know? Our notions of prayer also need turning upside down.

12 · Dominion and Power

From time to time a news item appears in the press telling how a group of parishioners have resisted the decision of the central authorities to close their church or recounting that a bishop or a committee is seeking to remove a minister from a charge in which he is causing distress and scandal. Mostly the reaction of people to the news items is one of shocked surprise that the church should be involved in such a battle.

'How unchristian,' they say. The assumption always is that the parties should not have got themselves into a state of conflict. Either the dissidents should have been persuaded to see the light, or authority should have compromised.

Such a view fails to recognize the level of determination in any human group which can be mobilized either to resist or impose authority. Yet it bears witness to the intrinsically true assumption that the gospel pattern of power is not like that of the world.

Every company of people must in one way or another have a structure to enable decisions to be taken, and must also have some way of dealing with its deviant minorities. As far as the latter goes, the traditional method has been to impose a form of ultimate sanction which ensures that, in the long term, opposition does not pay.

We accept that within a political or economic situation such must be the case. The state has always claimed the right to execute or imprison those who persist in rebellion. The courts sustain their authority in the last resort by punishing for contempt those who ignore their decisions. As another amongst the human institutions the church has also, from time to time, claimed the right of imposing sanctions upon those who would not accept its ruling. Yet always there has been a sense that this was out of keeping with its original spirit. While the secular lord might exact vengeance on his vassal, the spiritual authority of the bishop should only be displayed in love for those who were under his jurisdiction, and anything less caused a jarring note.

Such is certainly the ideal. Yet, one must ask how in practice any institution can remain unique in this respect, when it is set in history and has to maintain a relationship with the others which need a different form of power.

The church itself asks the same questions, and wriggles with embarrassment as its lawyers compose new canons, and argue that regulations must be given teeth. It is always vulnerable to the attack of critics who cite the tortures of the Inquisition or such instances as that of Thomas Becket who, as the Archbishop of Canterbury in exile, ceremonially excommunicated his political opponents.

While the gospel declares a new way, the church is composed of sinful human beings. Its members also belong to the other organizations, political and social, so there are bound to be assumptions which are carried across from one to the other. This can be a healthy cross-fertilization but there is always the danger that the church will conform to secular principles, rather than mirror the gospel.

Beside the question of how the church is structured internally, there is also that of how it is interacting with society at large. Just as there is a problem of how a leader can also be a servant, so the church corporately has to find a way of changing society in the direction of the kingdom without making a bid for domination.

A fresh approach to the use of power is of urgent practical relevance to our present political situation. Within almost every country there is a question of who rules and by what authority. Internationally the traditionally weaker nations are discovering their power in an increasingly inter-related world.

There is everywhere a revolt against any attempt to impose an external conformity even when the purpose is demonstrably benevolent. The poor countries are exploring the possibility of using their raw materials as a way of breaking the economic dominance of the industrialized world. The workers are holding to ransom the traditional wielders of power in the developed societies. Everywhere the individual with a grievance has become aware that the technology of destruction can put into his hand devices which give him power over the lives of others and through them he can blackmail authority.

The game of dominance – the perception of the other as a pawn at the disposal of the more powerful – is fast proving unworkable. In such a context the alternative thinking provided by the gospel begins to take on a new aspect. It also claims power but along lines that once again turn our traditional notions upside down, and call in question the accepted patterns of church practice that we have been noticing in this chapter.

So leaving aside all the paraphernalia of church government to which we have grown accustomed, let us go back to the New Testament and enquire about the power of the gospel.

In the opening paragraphs of his Letter to the Romans Paul mentions the gospel twice, preaching the gospel once; and then he continues, as if in explanation of this: 'For I am not ashamed of the gospel: it is the power of God for salvation to everyone who has faith' (Rom. 1.16).

He had said before that it was the gospel of God, and the gospel of his Son. It is, he means, the good news that God declares about his Son, and thus about what is available in his Son. He is now saying that what is available is salvation, the way in which it is available is through faith; and, because God is the author of it, the gospel is as powerful as God. This is why Paul is not ashamed of the gospel, but eager to preach it to those who are in Rome.

The power of the gospel is in the forefront of Paul's thinking. He refers to it again, at the end of the letter:

> I will not venture to speak of anything except what Christ has wrought through me to win obedience from the Gentiles, by word and deed, by the power of signs and wonders, by the power of the Holy Spirit, so that from Jerusalem as far round as Illyricum I have fully preached the gospel of Christ (Rom. 15.18f.).

When Paul preached the gospel, signs and wonders followed, and the Holy Spirit demonstrated his power. In Paul's mouth, the gospel was a word of power. Paul was reflecting on this, as he turned from his mission to the Eastern part of the Mediterranean to prepare for his visit to the West, and wrote this letter.

When we remember what was achieved through Paul, we can see how it was that he came to think of the gospel as powerful. And when we recall other preachers in that century, and in later centuries, we see the same results. The gospel certainly has been a powerful message in the past; the question is, is it powerful today? And if it is not, is that because of some uncertainty as to what the gospel is; and hence another reason for asking, What is the gospel?

Once more we come to the fact that the gospel cannot be formulated; that is, expressed in a formula. If it could be, we should only need to enquire what Paul or Aidan or Francis or Ignatius Loyola or John Wesley or some other preacher said, and say it again in his words. But we know that if we were to do that, we should find that the power had gone out of the words; that would not be my gospel. Every evangelist must find his own form of expression for the gospel.

Another way of saying this is that the gospel is the power of God; therefore it cannot be controlled by man, or placed at his disposal. The preacher himself must first be overpowered by the gospel, before he can preach it to others with power. Otherwise it would not be the power of God, but the power of man.

This is a twofold activity; it has a negative side, and a positive side. The negative is breaking down and rooting up; the positive, building up and planting. The gospel is the power by which God breaks down and builds up, destroying the evil in the present order, and saving his creation for the new age.

Destruction and salvation is a major theme in Mark's gospel; Jesus is presented as one who destroys the demons and saves those who are at their mercy. This is the reason why Mark's gospel is so rich in miracle stories: miracles of exorcism express the power of the gospel to break down and build up. What the demon's say in Mark's gospel is meant to be taken seriously. As James says, 'The demons believe' (James 2.19); they know what is what. The first demon to speak in Mark tells the reader what Jesus has come to do, and he is speaking the truth: 'You have come to destroy us' (Mark 1.24 NEB mg).

The context in which he says this is important (Mark 1.21–28); the demon is in a synagogue. The story has a double theme: Jesus and the unclean spirits; and, Jesus and the Jews. He confronts the unclean spirits with his power to destroy them: and he confronts the Jews with new teaching with authority. Or one could say that the story has a single theme: Jesus releases men from bondage; both the bondage of the religious law and the bondage of the devil. Mark, unlike Matthew, believed that Jesus had come to destroy the law (contrast Matt. 5.17).

This is why Mark has conflict stories as well as miracle stories in his gospel: the miracle stories show Jesus as the destroyer of the devil and his minions, the demons or unclean spirits; the conflict stories, in which Jesus argues with the religious leaders, show Jesus as the destroyer of the law. According to Mark, a man is saved not by keeping the law, but by faith in Jesus the Saviour: 'Your faith has saved you' (Mark 5.34; 10.52).

Mark expresses destruction and salvation in a dramatic form; or rather, that is how it looks to us, because we do not believe in demons in the way he did. We must therefore look for another way of thinking about the destructive and saving power of the gospel – a way that will make sense today. How does the gospel destroy, and how does it save?

The gospel destroys by telling us that the society to which we are happy to belong is under the power of evil, and that to be a friend to this society is to be an enemy of God (James 4.4). It tells us that the treasure we are laying up will be moth-eaten, and will rust away (Matt. 6.19). It devalues all those things that we had thought valuable. Anyone who believed the gospel would find that what used to attract him and hold him in its grip did so no longer. Status, success and security would lose their power over him. Moreover, what attracts now also inevitably divides. Status has no meaning, unless there are people of a lower standing on whom one can look down. Success is nothing, if all win and have prizes; success entails the failure of the unsuccessful. Security is only attractive in an insecure situation, when others lack it. The gospel destroys the goals that divide, and presents the possibility of fellowship: the fellowship of the gospel. It saves men for one another, from competition into a community that is non-competitive. The gospel comes with power to make the members of the new society, destroying the old, with its divisions and injustices, and opening up the new life of fellowship and love.

The gospel is the power of God, and is never the power of man, at man's disposal. It is God's power, and it is always

68

exercised for God's purpose. But this should make us think about it once more.

How does God do things? Never the way we do them. His thoughts and his ways are as far from ours as earth is from heaven. We are back with our formula for inverting our natural way of thinking to conform with the gospel way. Once again, in the case of power we must change the sign outside the bracket. God's power is not like man's.

Power suggests something irresistible, such as the wind at gale force, or a bursting dam, or high voltage electricity. Power is that which cannot be opposed, and is seen as such. But in the case of God's power, it is just the opposite; here, power is manifested in weakness.

We preach Christ crucified, a stumbling block to Jews and folly to Gentiles, but to those who are called, both Jews and Greeks, Christ the power of God and the wisdom of God (I Cor. 1.23f.).

The power of God is manifested in a crucified Messiah; that is to say in powerlessness and weakness. God manifests his power, and exercises his power, in and through its opposite: weakness.

The same is the case with the man who believes and preaches the gospel. He is not a powerful person, but precisely the opposite. He shares in the sufferings of Christ, and he must lose his life in order to save it.

Mark makes this clear in his gospel; he shows the powerlessness of Jesus, and of the disciple. Jesus destroys the demons and Judaism, but only by being destroyed. The sign of the end of the law is the rending of the curtain in the temple, but this is not recorded until after the death of Jesus (Mark 15.38; contrast Luke 23.45). His power to destroy lies only in being destroyed. And so with the disciples; the possibility of their being saved depends on their not saving themselves (Mark 8.34f.).

The gospel is the power of God and by it he is making the new world in which righteousness dwells. But it is not power in human terms; looked at from the human point of view, it is weakness and folly. The gospel creates the people of the new world, but they are not powerful in terms of this world; their power now is their weakness: 'For when I am weak, then I am strong' (II Cor. 12.10).

This is the essential risk of the gospel, because it is the risk of loving. In that you make yourself vulnerable, you renounce your rights. This is dangerous enough between two persons. What happens when it becomes a wider way of life? By definition it has let go the sanctions of power as we know them and so can always be pilloried as folly or suppressed as a scandal. It has no remedy for such treatment. There is no warrant in it for guerilla tactics to be employed in its own cause (which does not rule out the possibility that it might be right to apply them on behalf of the oppressed). There is only the faith that out of ultimate loss resurrection will come.

If this fresh understanding of the gospel is to be applied in the present crisis of power, the church must provide some kind of demonstration or witness which will carry conviction. The joy of finding a way through the contemporary frustration will be real; but equally there must be a realistic understanding of what that way involves.

The church which is the embodiment of such a gospel has got to face the possibility of the death and resurrection pattern being worked out for its own self as an institution. When this has happened in the past it has appeared in the form of persecution; the threat has been external. Now the choice concerns the church's own understanding of its power and status. Christians have enjoyed centuries of social acceptance, their leaders have taken their places among the great of the land, their buildings have achieved the prestige of Solomon's Temple and still rank high in the tourist attractions of Western Europe. The Moderator of the General Assembly or the bishop of a diocese visiting a military establishment will be accorded the honours of a senior officer. Is this how it should be or does all this need to pass through the sea-change of repentance?

Before we can consider such a question we will have to look again at our self-understanding as churchmen. Congregations of Christians meeting for Sunday worship have often felt themselves to be the support group of the larger institution – 'our denomination' or 'our diocese'. In fact the gospel priority would seem to be the other way round. The essential core of the 'church event' is the meeting of Christians in the presence of the risen Jesus. This is the one thing that matters. All the rest of the church organization and its structures exist only to enable that experience to occur, to be sustained and to be shared ever more widely. But what the disciples found in Jesus' company did not square with the way that the rest of the world ran its organizations. So John pictures the Last Supper with the master reversing roles and washing his disciples' feet and makes the contrast explicit. So Paul in both letters to the Corinthians emphasizes the point in different images (see I Cor. 1.26–31, II Cor. 6.4–10).

How does such a church operate, and how does it relate to other organizations? If it remains true to its original pattern, the forms of leadership that it produces will raise profound questions about every other kind of authority. For much of its history, however, the church has conformed to the patterns of society around. When James VI of Scotland and I of England made his famous observation 'No bishop, no king', he was arguing that the same political forces which were against church hierarchy would ultimately oppose the idea of monarchy as well. His experience had given him no reason to see the church in any different light from the rest of society's institutions.

This is totally at variance with the New Testament view of the church. Once the company of believers have become identified with a culture, they may produce the odd comment upon prevailing morality but they cannot express that radical comment upon the basic assumptions of the whole order which needs to come from the gospel. The Lord who puts down the mighty from their seat and exalts the humble and meek requires servants whose prophetic role goes beyond a distaste for pornography or a praiseworthy desire to promote better housing.

Among the Western nations we are used to church meetings where we anxiously examine the falling graphs of church membership. So far we have mostly assumed that the appropriate response is to call in the stewardship advisers to help bolster things up or lay on a mission. Behind this lies the hope that if we can find the right note to strike the numbers of adherents will return and things can go on as before. The church will again take its place in national life, relating to the power structures, as it did in the 'good old days'. But it may be that society needs the prophetic leadership which will help it change rather than a refurbished church which will go on maintaining, funding and administering the existing machinery.

We might take the example of a new town. There is an

immediate assumption by church people at every level that the gospel will necessarily be promoted by owning a building in which services can be conducted. There may be those who hold to another theory, but the majority view inevitably carries the day, because the expectations of laity and clergy alike are too strong. An experimental ministry may be started but as Christians gather they begin to feel a need for a place which is recognizably a 'church' in traditional terms, and with undeniable enthusiasm they work to raise funds for it. Then the body of Christians formed round it begins to see itself as one among many groups to be represented on local committees, to share in fund raising opportunities with the Lifeboat, the Red Cross and so on. The church is once again firmly anchored in the *status quo*.

There can always be the danger that too radical a theology may seem to be imposing its point of view on others. You cannot in the name of the gospel bludgeon someone else into submission. There can be no exemption for any point of view from the rule that the gospel as an idea must never be imposed at the expense of the individual. The claim of those who want to look for new church structures is that these would free the gospel. In support of this view they can cite the people outside the present church who have rejected it as cramping or unmeaningful. Yet there are others to whom it is a life-sustaining resource.

The tug-of-war between radicals and traditionalists has been felt in every denomination. Too often the opposing views have been upheld by manoeuvres of ecclesiastical politics. Authorities have been quoted by either side. The only question to ask by way of guidance is 'Where is the presence of Jesus?' Where he is, the gospel will be heard and dead men will live. That will be the place where the church is renewed.

Where such renewal takes place, there is always an experience or irrepressible life. It does not have to be defended with careful structures. Where Christians become obsessed with the survival of the church or claiming for it power or authority, the Spirit has gone. The gospel call is then to go out into the wilderness to find him again.

But the gospel is not given in order that the church may be a model institution, but that all men may have new life. The church exists so that the world may believe and in believing, operate in a new way. So it is at the frontiers of operation between the church and the other structures of society that the gospel must be given effective form. There is no other single question which is so urgent today as that of authority. Among individuals, in society and in the community of nations every accepted form of power-based leadership is being challenged. As never before the church is needed to demonstrate in action that authority which comes from love, which gives each individual his due, and leads him by the way of service into love of others. It is not a theory which can be applied in a detached way. It is a gospel of redemption to be lived by fallen men, based on the faith that there is available God's Spirit to achieve in us his excessive, scandalous yet joyful, loving will.

13 · Make it Happen!

Confronted with some sorts of information or given new insights, it is sufficient to say 'How interesting'. A declaration of the gospel is not like that, it demands action.

If what we have tried to expound in this book is true, then something ought to be done about it. If, on the other hand, it is felt that we have distorted the gospel then something also needs to be done about that, at least by way of refutation.

Leaving the second option to others, all we can do is turn our attention to the first. If we have seen clearly, what then must be done?

Talk of reform and renewal has been in the air for twenty years and more. Ginger groups like The Servants of Christ the King have found a few devoted adherents but left the main structure of church life untouched. The charismatic movement makes its appeal largely to those of a particular temperament and lays its emphasis upon experience rather than looking for a new shape to the church and society.

The Church of England has sought to reorganize its pattern of decision-making through synodical government but, at least as it is experienced by the ordinary church members, and even more when observed by other from outside, it seems to have achieved something less than a new outpouring of the Spirit.

None of the changes have reversed the downward trend of church membership. Indeed some of the busyness of reorganization seems designed to distract attention from such basic facts. When that defence is not used and the decreasing graph is acknowledged, the next response is to look round for external causes upon which to lay the blame. Television, the educational system, the motor cars which take all the family out on Sunday have all in their turn been cited as causes of the declining practice of religion.

Others look within the churches themselves to find a source of the ills. A despairing writer in *Blackwood's Magazine* around 1970 diagnosed causes which included those clergy who did not uphold the Ten Commandments, the theology of Bishop John Robinson and the New English Bible! All too seldom, at the popular level, is there ever a question as to whether the church as we know it, in whatever denomination, has failed to be an effective incarnation of the gospel and so left the world without the model by which it might understand the kind of salvation which could meet its need. One of the great disappointments, expressed in a variety of ways, is that the church in spite of all that it stands for does not 'look redeemed'.

What would be needed by way of change in the local congregation if it were going to give such an impression? At first sight people are tempted to answer the question in terms of harmony, lack of conflict and mutual understanding and then to move on to a programme of good works. This is to set a course for the church which will end by making it a sect of the devout, dedicated to the game of disguising their real feelings.

The twelve around Jesus were certainly not like that. They were quarrelling about status at the Last Supper; Peter after his flash of inspiration in acknowledging the messiahship of Jesus returned to the banality of a very human fear of pain and, when he voiced it, found himself rebuked as the devil. The young church at Corinth was not a utopian body of well-adjusted churchmen. They produced almost every sort of deviancy for Paul to rebuke. They were factious, they took each other to court, they indulged in grave sexual misdemeanours, they had no manners at the eucharist, their conduct of worship was enthusiastic but disorderly. As he writes to them, however, Paul gives us a clue which maybe can help us in our practical problems in finding a strategy for action.

We discover in chapter 15 of the first Letter to the Corinthians that for Paul the key to the gospel is the resurrection. Many a churchman today might well feel that this was one of the least practical parts of his belief. A comfort to the bereaved perhaps, but something that is best left on one side, except for Easter Day.

Paul's argument is very different from this. All he has written to the Corinthians about their conduct of church life, his vision

75

of how they might be united instead of separated and his great hymn about love, find their culmination in the chapter on the resurrection. We are accustomed to thinking of this as something which happened to Jesus and quite how it happened we are often hard put to say. Paul sees the resurrection as something that happens to all of us. His argument makes it quite clear that he is not discussing the experience of the risen Jesus as being part of his divinity. When we take that point of view we say, 'Well of course it happened to him because he was the Son of God.' By contrast, Paul's argument follows the line: 'It happened to one of us, so the breakthrough has occurred and we now know as a result that we can share in this.'

This has nothing to do with a belief in man's automatic immortality. That idea sees the soul as the kind of indestructible diamond encased in a rather inadequate plastic setting. The implication is that when the body falls away, and the mind too, there is still something left which we call a 'soul' and it has an intrinsic survival value. What that thing might be when all the aspects of an individual represented by mind and body are discarded is hard to imagine since every distinguishing mark will have gone. The Christian doctrine of the resurrection is that after death the whole personality which through all the years of a man's life is both expressed by his body and also finds meaning and understanding through mind and imagination is, by the action of God who originated the gift of life, brought together again in its wholeness in a new mode of being.

If we can accept this as a real hope, then we are saved from holding on despairingly to the past because we cannot picture any alternative mode of being.

This is what happens to people who mourn and in their grief try to recreate the personality that was. They may keep the physical arrangements of a familiar room untouched, as Queen Victoria did with Prince Albert; they may surround themselves with photographs; their imagination may recreate a sense of the presence of the departed in an accustomed place to ease the sense of loss. Doubtless the distraught disciples would have liked Jesus back again after Good Friday as they had known him in the days of his flesh. That is specifically denied – 'Don't cling to me,' says the Lord in the garden to Mary of Magdala. By contrast, in the resurrection appearances, the evangelists are struggling to write an alternative scenario describing the risen presence in language which continually proves inadequate. In just the same way Paul in the Letter to the Corinthians is reduced to complicated speculations about 'a spiritual body', made all the more difficult for us to understand since it is woven in with his mistaken expectation of the Lord's return within the lifetime of at least some of his readers (I Cor. 15. 51f.).

When we have disentangled the core of this resurrection hope it amounts to the revolutionary belief in the possibility of an 'alternative scenario'. Once we have grasped this principle we discover that it is not something which is applicable only to the idea of physical death and new life for the individual. It is the pattern by which the believer is called to live all his days.

Every occasion of the breaking of bread was a statement by the first Christians that they lived in the presence of the Lord who was risen. They partook of his new life and therefore, being 'in Christ' they were experiencing a new mode of being, a new creation. That is to say they were living in the world of the 'alternative scenario'.

This is the world where you are no longer a prisoner of the past, because you believe you can look for the new thing that will replace it. This attitude is what we need in planning for the future.

The first necessity for any new strategy is a changed expectation of how the church is meant to exist in the world. If in a time of difficulties such as the present the survival of the institution occupies all the energy of churchmen, then we may detect the writing on the wall. Just like Peter urging his Lord to play safe and avoid the crunch, the church dedicated to preserving itself speaks not with the prophetic voice from God, but in the tones of demonic self-centredness. It will become one more 'good cause' frantically appealing for money and quickly jealous of those in the beggars' queue who seem to do better.

Moreover a time of financial stringency challenges the church to shape itself in new ways so that it can be a sign to the world where self-interest and rivalry will increasingly dominate the scene.

As we write this there are growing evidences of the deep divisions in British society which seem destined to prevent any attempt to solve our national problems on the basis of an appeal to 'one nation'. But beyond this difficulty, which may perhaps be short-term, there remains the question of the sharing of mankind's resources between the rich nations and the poor. The gospel is essentially good news for the poor. Can it be declared by the church which always seems identified with the affluent and the powerful?

Through the centuries the church has found renewal through movements which in a representative way have reaffirmed the identification of the gospel with the poor. The origins of monasticism, the rise of the friars, the witness of Methodism, were all attempts to express the pattern of death and resurrection, to challenge the assumptions of the world about power and success and were therefore attempts to write an alternative scenario.

What is needed within our own situation? We are not without a number of movements which bear the gospel marks of newness, offence, excess, joy and love. They exist within the Roman Catholic church in such examples as the Little Brothers of Charles de Foucauld, in the Focolari movement and many others. In Britain Christian communities have sprung up, not modelled on the earlier forms of the religious life but on living together, seeking new forms of spirituality and simpler lifestyles. We may rejoice at these manifestations of new life, but what is happening in the local congregations where the ordinary life of the church finds expression? For it is here that the most important changes must come.

In many places devoted clergy and people spend their energies trying to make the inherited system work. By their friendliness they encourage people to join their congregation, newcomers are welcomed in, the lapsed are visited and urged to return. But what they are offered is precisely the same church from which they lapsed. Even supposing they respond to the invitation, will they find themselves in the kind of meeting which actually enables individuals to experience the truth of the gospel? Or will such elementary matters as the arrangement of the seating or the size of the gathering make the whole operation virtually impossible from the start? If Christians come to agree that different ways of worship are needed, what are they going to do about it? Are the congregations which can still keep going with a respectable number at worship on a Sunday morning going to risk disturbing their 'successful' patterns? Or must we always wait till a Christian group begins to dwindle before any experiment is tried?

Up to the present, even that has not been the way of things. Church strategy has been to amalgamate two falling congregations into what is hoped will be one viable unit designed to operate exactly as before. But what is to prevent this going the way of its two predecessors? There is a danger that 'practical ecumenism' may also advance upon the same mistaken assumption that smaller worshipping units might best be amalgamated to share one building or one minister.

Resurrection is not about keeping the organs functioning once the spirit is dead. That is the approach of mechanistic medicine which tries to manipulate even death. Faith lets go in trust and waits for the free gift of new life.

So what do we do in the institutional church? First there must be a recognition that this is a time for choosing a way forward rather than standing still in the hope that, of their own volition, things will get better. Following this, a realistic system of priorities must be established in relation to the activities of church members, the use of the professional manpower of the church and the way that property and plant are handled. Intelligent lay people have commented how much energy is expended on maintaining an organization which raises funds to maintain an organization. No wonder they sometimes become disheartened.

If radical reassessment of priorities is to be attempted both at congregational level and by the leadership of the churches, all concerned must be prepared to put all thought of safety first out of their considerations. They must concentrate on the question how Christians can be encouraged in their prime objective of meeting together for worship and above all for the breaking of bread. If that is seen as the priority, then a ministerial pattern must be developed which makes this possible. We may have to find new and unpaid leadership within the local Christian cell. This may mean thinking out afresh how those who are to preside at the eucharist should be equipped and trained and what due authorization will mean for such a ministry. Academic discussions of such issues can be protracted over years. New forms are needed now, and as they are undertaken, the real theological issues will emerge.

Experiments in ministry are always surrounded by uncertainties and questions, often voiced by the clergy. These sometimes sound like a professional body anxiously safe-guarding its status. Any suggestion of introducing men into the ordained priesthood through channels other than the academically respectable ones of the past is met with slogans about 'mass priests' and the dilution of standards. The picture seems so often to be that of the graduate in the pulpit. Instead ministry ought to have as its model the picture of a man pouring water into a bowl and washing his disciples' dusty feet. It is an activity undertaken to meet a recognized need and to declare God's loving kindness towards the world he loves.

Such a view must govern our understanding of the church hierarchy as well as the local ministry. There is room for new life-styles within the church with barriers of formality coming down. It is sometimes said that there is no problem about this, but are we not blinded by custom to the things we do? What does the enthronement of a diocesan bishop really say to onlookers about the chief pastor of the area? What sort of gospel would you expect to hear emerging from a General Assembly where the chairman wears lace ruffles and knee breeches and the whole attendant court of Lord High Commissioner, purse bearer and ladies-in-waiting might well come from a Gilbert and Sullivan opera?

But if these are out-dated forms, no longer speaking a living word in our generation, what do we do? Where does change begin? Reform does not come by itself. It happens when individuals have the courage to challenge the norms. It requires an honest facing of priorities – as Jesus did over and over again with the churchmen of his day.

Whoever takes a stand that puts a question mark against what society accepts, will find himself under considerable pressure. The loneliness of disapproval can shake the self-esteem which each of us needs to survive, and bring a man to the point where he mistrusts the course he is following. Mutual support and the reassurance of friends become extremely important. If the individual believer is to be encouraged to follow the leading of the gospel into these dangerous areas, he will need the kind of fellowship and intimacy in which he can find both a critical appraisal of his insights and the certainty of support as he tries to give expression to them. If we are concerned about the church we need to become involved in the kind of group which takes seriously the possibility of action for change.

Whenever one tries to suggest a detailed course of action apart from a concrete situation two dangers appear. First, any list of things to be done appears trivial or else irrelevant to another person's problems. Secondly, one falls quickly into the trap of promoting a 'programme' which becomes an end in itself.

What needs to happen in our present situation must begin with a shift in the churches' self-understanding. In every denomination there are the same uncriticized assumptions about the way that the institution ought to survive. They arise out of a thousand years in which church and society have been closely interwoven. Events are challenging these assumptions and in addition the question has to be faced whether the gospel also demands the reshaping which is likely to be forced upon us. In that case the loss of prestige, the withering away of investments from the past, may become a positive gain and not a crippling blow. Once again the good news is that we are set free into the Now and prohibited from living with backward glances, sighing 'If only . . .!'

This means also a new attitude to the events which shape our lives. As members of our society we live with continual comments upon rising prices, and a longing for the days when as a whole our nation was part of the world's minority who could be told that 'we had never had it so good'. All around us is the determination to make sure that if things get difficult, our own group, whatever that may be, will take precautions to ensure that we are insulated against the worst of the shock.

This is a recipe for political and economic strife. When everyone is anxiously defending his or her own rights, justice quickly gets forgotten and it is difficult to be an advocate for the interests of others without appearing a traitor to one's own grouping.

If the gospel is applied in the field of political confrontation it takes a person out of the sterotyped role of a party member. It asserts that all concerned are equally the children of God. If this can be accepted then there comes a liberation from the pressure of other allegiances. We are set free to move with hope into a new set of circumstances in which we can respond.

In the present situation this may mean that we will accept that it is only equitable for us to have a lower standard of living if by this means other people in the world may get a fairer share. If this can be seen as a response to the gospel, there will not be any sense of failure or resentment but rather an ease and a joy about the simpler life-style that we have assumed. Instead of feeling impoverished we may find that our scale of priorities has changed and that there is more time for growth as persons, less emphasis upon status achieved by possessions or success. The insight of the gospel will turn our loss into gain.

If action is to follow our glimpse of the gospel it is certain that it will not be thought eminently sensible by the world. It is unlikely to be a popular movement within the whole church. Instead we may expect to find experiments which act as prophetic signs, rejected at first but gradually accepted in a way that shifts the consciousness of the institution towards the insight of the gospel. Then the experiment itself will become institutionalized, the free action of grace will be trapped in the rules of a game and a new reformation will be necessary. The people concerned will need to hear the gospel again in all its freshness. This must have been the painful experience of the first friars who gathered round Francis of Assisi. They could never say 'We've made it'; he was always moving on to new experiences, just as he was always giving away his cloak when his followers thought they had got him safely provided with warmth for the winter!

The areas most continually in need of the gospel's unsettling are those that buttress the institution, such as property and wealth, status without and hierarchy within. Yet these form the essence of ordered living. To turn these upside-down seems to invite chaos; it frightens us.

A canon of an ancient cathedral is said to have used the Prayer Book version of the Prayer of Humble Access with the Freudian inversion 'thou art the same Lord whose mercy is always to have property'. There speaks the institution; but God's mercy is at work continually to break us open to new life and to show us ways in which we can find support from our fellow Christians in pursuing it.

14 · Practical Politics

Through hearing the gospel our values are turned upside down: we see God, the world, power and a whole host of other things in a new way. To live with such insight, we have suggested, believers need one another. Church membership provides the context in which it is possible to take the gospel seriously and put it into practice. But there we again run into difficulty because the church which is meant to be the expression of the gospel also continually needs to be reformed by the gospel in its own right. There must necessarily be a tension for Christians between the need for internal reform in the light of the gospel and the task of declaring the gospel to the world. It might be said that we have concentrated too much in this book on the former and only spoken of the latter by implication. Yet the church exists for the sake of the world and therefore we cannot be content with any description of its task which falls short of the purpose of universal salvation. How can we translate what has been said about the gospel into terms which make it applicable to all men everywhere?

One of the fundamental concerns which face thinking people today is the future of mankind. On the one hand there seem to open out ahead vistas of immense possibilities. Human achievement has pushed back the boundaries of space with moon shots and inter-planetary probes; we have enlarged the boundaries of life by our medical skills and by the expertise of the behavioural sciences we have expanded our awareness of one another. In such a world there is room for tremendous optimism about the future. Out of such an approach comes writing like the following:

It has often been noted that a characteristic of contemporary man is that he lives in terms of tomorrow, oriented towards the future, fascinated by what does not yet exist. The spiritual condition of today's man is more and more determined by the model of the man of tomorrow. Man's awareness of himself is heavily affected by the knowledge that he is outgrowing his present condition and entering a new era, a world 'to the second power' fashioned by his own hands. We live on the verge of man's epiphany, his 'anthropophany.' History is no longer, as it was for the Greeks, an *anamnesis*, a remembrance. It is rather a thrust into the future. The contemporary world is full of latent possibilities and expectations. History seems to have quickened its pace. The confrontation of the present with the future makes man impatient.

Matching this optimism is another point of view acutely aware of all the dangers that threaten us. Following this line we learn that planet Earth carries already far too many inhabitants and they are increasing at a rate which can only mean disaster unless it is checked; food supplies are at risk; we are facing an energy crisis and perhaps a breakdown of our whole economic system. Within such a situation human beings tend to revert to savage techniques of self-preservation leading to political chaos. This could spell total destruction in a world where a proliferation of nuclear capability has given the opportunity for less and less responsible groups to threaten their numerically more powerful enemies and to blur the discrimination between heroic defiance and naked terrorism.

The gospel turns upside down the brash self-confidence of technological man and calls in question his assumption of salvation by efficiency. But it also turns through 180° the despair of those who feel the overwhelming complexity and dangers that lie ahead.

The men who live by the gospel are called to penetrate the world; as they take their part in all its life their task will be to raise the questions which their faith demands. At the point of self-congratulation by the group or party with which they are involved, they may need to call attention to the cost at which the 'success' has been achieved. It may be that the cause has triumphed at the expense of individual integrity or the good of another set of interests. It may be that in their achievement the reformers are in danger of joining the power game and becoming part of the evil they sought to combat. The witnesses to the gospel will find they are turning their easy assumptions upside down.

The same will be true at the point where 'sensible people' can find no way forward. Where common sense sees a minus, the gospel puts a plus. It therefore makes sense to work amongst people whose humanity would otherwise have been written off in terms of practical politics. The gospel assumption is that Christ is disclosed in the unlikely person of the sick, the prisoner, the naked, when instead of being ignored he is taken seriously. It also looks for victory at the place of apparent defeat.

The politics of the world always make the mistake of taking the winners, the 'haves', the powerful, seriously. Yet by definition the losers are the majority and up till now a minority of 'haves' have existed by courtesy of a majority of 'have nots'. Revolution in its conventional sense simply reverses the pecking order. The gospel starts with the surprising assumption that all are powerless and needy and promises gifts to all on the basis of their weakness and failure. It may be that we cannot conceive a political life which operates by taking the powerless seriously. At least the witness of the gospel is needed in every political structure to point to that alternative possibility.

At first it may sound like romantic idealism, but there is a sense in which it is becoming increasingly clear that government at every level has got to take seriously the underprivileged whom it might be convenient to forget. The alternative is a totalitarian regime which can only exist by repression. As the technology of destruction puts physical violence more easily within reach of the oppressed, the issues become increasingly stark. Either mankind must begin to turn its ideas of power upside down or it will embark on an ever more violent course when rulers and ruled both stand to lose their humanity. The changed circumstances of our present situation make it urgent to take seriously the politics of a kingdom of heaven as a way of handling a technologically conditioned world.

This is no programme for a successful campaign to promote the gospel. As members of the institutional church we probably all entertain a lurking hope that something will turn up which so manifestly vindicates our message that all men of good sense will come flooding in. But the gospel is not for men of good sense or

85

good will who perceive themselves as such; it is for acknow-ledged sinners and that is not a popular or appealing self-image.

An understanding of the gospel will send its adherents into the world to be the salt, the leaven. They will not seek to capture the world for their institution so that it may become powerful, but will try to provide the stimulus which challenges every kind of system – political party, international corporation, trade union or cultural movement – and seek to lead it to repentance.

This cannot be done by a confrontation from without. The bishops and the barons standing against the mediaeval king were both of a kind even though they couched their cause in different language. They were all playing the game of power. Only the fool who nestles at the king's feet can slip in the word of wis-dom, the uncomfortable advice, which can be heard because it has no threat of domination in it. Here is the most appropriate model for the church and for the individual Christian, speaking the foolishness of God's truth from a position which threatens nobody's status.

We set out to hunt the gospel. We find it where perhaps we knew all along it would be, in a person or company of people who have about them the weak innocence of the child. The people who are wise because they are capable of asking the foolishly direct question. The people who are rich because they do not possess anything whose loss can destroy them; the saints who know themselves to be sinners. Maddening people whose love and insight may save the world, but whom no one would dream of wanting for Prime Minister! People whose message seems wildly impractical but who have an urgent task to perform in ensuring the sanity, perhaps also the survival of the political life of mankind, in any recognizable human form.

Notes

Chapter 2

1. G. K. Chesterton, *Orthodoxy*, 1909; Collins Fontana ed. 1960, p. 159.

Chapter 3

1. Pirke Aboth 4.13. See R. H. Charles, *Apocrypha and Pseudepigrapha*, Vol. 11, Clarendon Press 1913, p. 705.
2. 4 Macc. 17, 20–22; ibid, p. 683.
3. T. S. Eliot, *Little Gidding* in *Four Quartets*, Faber & Faber 1944, p. 39.

Chapter 6

1. Alan Moorehead, *Darwin and the 'Beagle'*, Hamish Hamilton 1969; Penguin Books 1971, p. 37.
2. Sydney Carter, 'Come Holy Harlequin' from *Green Print for Song*, Galliard 1974. Used by permission of Stainer & Bell Ltd.

Chapter 14

1. Gustavo Gutierrez, *A Theology of Liberation*, SCM Press 1974, p. 213.